EASY JAMS, CHUTNEYS
AND PRESERVES

ABOUT THE AUTHORS

Val and John Harrison live in the north-west of England. They grow their own fruit and vegetables on two allotments which provide the ingredients for the homemade jams, chutneys and preserves they have enjoyed making for over 30 years.

John runs two popular websites **www.lowcostliving.co.uk** and **www.allotment.org.uk** and is the author of three bestselling books in the *Right Way* series: **Vegetable Growing Month by Month, The Essential Allotment Guide** and **Low-Cost Living.**

EASY JAMS, CHUTNEYS AND PRESERVES

Val and John Harrison

RIGHT WAY

Constable & Robinson Ltd
3 The Lanchesters
162 Fulham Palace Road
London W6 9ER
www.constablerobinson.com

This edition published by Right Way,
an imprint of Constable & Robinson, 2009

Copyright © Val and John Harrison, 2009

The rights of Val and John Harrison to be identified as the
authors of this work have been asserted by them in accordance
with the Copyright, Designs & Patents Act 1988.

A copy of the British Library Cataloguing in Publication Data
is available from the British Library

ISBN: 978-0-7160-2225-1

Printed and bound in the EU

7 9 10 8 6

CONTENTS

INTRODUCTION

In an age when most things are available straight off the supermarket shelf at a low price, you may wonder why it is worth the bother of making your own. After all, you can pick up a jar of jam or pickle easily enough in any supermarket. Well, just try to pick up a jar of chilli jam that adds both bite and sweetness to a cheese sandwich or lemon and mustard seed chutney to accompany grilled fish.

Commercially produced preserves always taste the same. They're working to absolutely standardized recipes: recipes that have been tried and tested to have the most appeal to the average consumer. Perhaps your taste is different from that of the average consumer in the focus group tested. Perhaps you want something a little different, a little spicier or fruitier. When you make your own you can have what you want.

With homemade preserves there is a certain amount of guesswork and instinct involved that improves with practice. It really is an art as much as a science. One of the joys of homemade is that element of luck. To be truthful, sometimes the results are just fair but sometimes your own preserves are absolutely wonderful. It's the difference between blended Euro-plonk wine and chateau bottled. One is always the same and acceptable but only the handmade is ever truly great.

Well, we've been making jams, chutneys and preserves at home for thirty years and our reasons for doing so are as valid today as when we started.

The first reason is simply quality. Yes, you can buy good

quality products but you have to look hard and long to find shop stocked preserves that are nearly as good as those you will make at home.

You are in total control of the ingredients and, for example, there is a difference in flavour between E331 sodium citrate and lemon juice in flavour even if they do the same job of providing acidity.

The second reason is cost. Often the base of our own product has cost nothing. A pleasant day blackberry picking results in pounds of jam for just the cost of the sugar; our pickled onions have cost little more than the vinegar, since we grow our own onions; and you can't even buy crab apples that our decorative tree donates in huge quantities for free each year.

The third reason is choice and individuality. When you buy from a shop, not only are you limited to what they stock but the products they do stock have been developed to please an average palette. Your own tastes will differ and you can cater for yourself.

If you like a bit of zing in your pickle you can add a chilli; if you like a lot you can add three. It's all a matter of what you like, not what is most acceptable to the average consumer.

The last of our reasons is definitely not least. It's fun and amazingly satisfying to make something yourself. Something unique and wonderful. To some degree it is, of course, a scientific process and when you start out it's best to stick exactly to the recipe but, as your skills and feeling for what you are doing develop, you begin to create your own recipes. You build on your understanding of the processes involved to become truly creative. Just in the same way that an artist will learn his craft, how to mix paints and stretch a canvas before creating a great painting, you learn the basics of the craft before making it into an art.

There are times when you will make mistakes and the end result will not be quite what you hoped or expected but 'nothing ventured, nothing gained'. We honestly cannot think of a 'failure' we've made that hasn't still been very palatable or at least acceptable.

Before you start, it's worth getting an exercise book and keeping a record of your preserves. Note down the recipe you use and what the final result was like. With chutneys where the full flavour isn't apparent immediately because they often take two or three months to mature, a note of what you did is really useful on the day you open the jar and taste the contents. Perhaps the flavour is a little mild or perhaps too hot but you will know next time from your little recipe book and notes.

If you get the home preserving bug, and we hope you do, then you will end up with more than you can eat at home, unless you have a very large family. The good news is that your homemade preserves make fantastic presents. One Christmas we found ourselves unusually well off and decided it was time we gave the family proper shop bought gifts. Well, we spent quite a bit of money and thought quite hard about what we picked for people only for them to be received with faint polite smiles. Then came the question, 'Have you stopped making chutney?' We think that speaks for itself.

One development since we started making our own preserves is that computers are more common now than telephones were then. Using a desktop publishing program you can easily create great labels for your products. You've always needed to note what's in the jar and importantly when it was made but now you can make it attractive as well.

Incidentally, you'll see in the recipes we recommend that you label the jars when fully cooled. There is a reason for this. We found that if you label the jars when hot the adhesive melts and the labels fall off.

The recipes in this book have been picked up over the years from books, magazines and, of course, friends and family and have been altered to suit our tastes. As we said before, don't

Fig. 1. Label for chilli jam.

be afraid to change things to suit your tastes once you have gained confidence.

We're a little old fashioned and work in proper pounds and ounces rather than decimal currency – however we've put the equivalent metric measures that will not affect the balance. Work in one system or the other – don't mix pints and kilograms in the same recipe or things will go wrong. It is the proportion of the ingredients to each other that matters more than the specific quantities.

An imperial teaspoon (abbreviation tsp) is a 5ml level measuring spoon and a tablespoon is a level 15ml metric measuring spoon. We've put a conversion chart at the end so you can convert any recipes you find, even American ones.

There are a lot of good (and some terrible) recipes out on the web but you'll find that our own website at **www.allotment.org.uk/recipes** has quite a few preserve recipes when you've made everything in this book!

Nowadays you can make preserves in small quantities using the microwave, in specialist jam making machines and even in some breadmakers. We've not included any specific recipes for these but have stuck with our traditional proven recipes that we know work well for the quantities most people make. As preserves store so well, it makes sense to make more rather than less.

One last point. When we started making our own jams and preserves, the recipe books available at that time were rather complicated. Full of equations and instructions for calculating how much sugar could be used for different fruits depending on acidity and pectin. Dire warnings abounded: under-boiling would result in non-setting but over-boiling would take you past the setting point. Some of the conserve recipes would take days of sugaring and transferring from one pan to another.

Well, when you both work and have children, you look for simple solutions because you just don't have the time to fuss and fiddle. We've kept this book straightforward and simple because this is how we do it.

Sometimes we bend and sometimes break the rules that we found in those old books, but the proof of the chutney is in the eating to mangle a phrase. Enjoy!

1

HISTORY OF MAKING PRESERVES

In our modern world with 24-hour shopping, cans in the cupboard and a deep freeze full of ready meals, it's hard to imagine the difficulties our ancestors had just keeping foods edible from harvest to harvest. Preserving food wasn't a hobby to them, it was literally a matter of survival!

The first people to record some of their methods were the Romans and they are known to have made jams to keep fruit for the winter. Fruit preserves are mentioned in Apicius or *On the subject of cooking*. Following the Fall of the Roman Empire and the Dark Ages in Europe we don't see any references to jams until the Crusaders return from the Middle East where it was still made.

It is possible to make jams using honey and other sweeteners but sugar is more convenient. When sugar first began to be imported from the colonies to Britain it was incredibly expensive but as the price fell it began to be used to make jams. Don't forget, apart from drying, it was the only way to preserve fruit for most people. It was very much a hit and miss affair, there was little understanding of sterilization and where moulds came from, so it was luck rather than judgement that decided if a jam would be good or a mouldy mess when the jar was opened.

Marmalades are similar to jams but the origin of the name itself has two attributions. The first is that the name comes from the Portuguese for quince, *marmelo* and early recipes for quince preserves did indeed call them marmalades.

The more romantic explanation goes back to Mary, Queen of Scots. The story is that her doctor prescribed a mixture of bitter oranges and sugar to help her with her sea sickness as she sailed from France to Scotland to reclaim her throne. One of her ladies in waiting who was making the mixture explained what she was doing as *'Marie est malade'* which became shortened to marmalade. Sadly, the first less romantic explanation is most probably the correct one.

Whilst jams came from the West, our chutneys came from the East. As Britain busily painted the globe red and occupied India they discovered the method of preserving known by the Hindi word *chatni*. It wasn't long before the idea was taken home, adapted and incorporated into our national cuisine. Unlike the reliance of jams on sugar for the preserving action, chutneys rely on a mixture of salt, vinegar, sugar and the anti-bacterial properties of the spices.

We think of the Victorians as staid people, yet they were very adventurous in their eating habits at least, absorbing Indian spices as if they'd always had them available. That most traditional British condiment, Piccalilli, dates right back to the middle of the eighteenth century, with the first recipes being for 'Indian Pickle or Piccalillo' in 1747. It made us smile to see a jar of 'Traditional Lancashire Piccalilli' – no doubt it should be washed down with traditional Yorkshire tea harvested from the plantations in the Dales.

Even our ketchup was an import from China and the Far East although the tomato ketchup that you find in every kitchen was more an American invention. It's amazing how global influences created our cuisine before anyone had heard the word globalization.

Unlike nowadays where chutneys and pickles tend to be a condiment, in those days before canned foods and refrigeration they provided the vegetable portion of a dish. Ham, bread and piccalilli would form a reasonably balanced meal and, since a chutney could contain a number of different vegetables and fruits, even meet the '5 A Day' requirements!

Initially a major problem in storing chutneys was the lack of suitable jars. It is important that air is completely excluded or the contents spoil. Various clay pots would be used and lids placed over or corks inserted and sealed with everything from candle wax to lard.

One common method was to stretch a soaked pig's bladder over the jar, which would create an airtight seal as it dried and shrunk onto the jar or pot. By the mid nineteenth century the Kilner and Mason jars were developed and marketed, bringing a method of reliably sealing out the air and foods became a lot easier and, more importantly, safer to produce and store at home.

Following the Second World War and the end of rationing in the 1950s, the home preserving of foods in Britain began to decline. The growth of cheap, mass-market foods accelerated this decline but now it's enjoying a resurgence as people rediscover the pleasure of creation and individuality in the kitchen.

2

HYGIENE AND HOW PRESERVING WORKS

One question we're frequently asked is, 'Can I use less sugar in my jam?' We think the question is prompted by concerns over consumption of sugar especially with regards to obesity. There's no doubt that sugar and salt are added to many processed foods with no justification other than improving and masking the flavour – or lack of it – of inferior products. With jams the sugar is generally vital to a successful result.

Having said that, you can make low sugar jams but they tend not to be as well set and need to be kept in the fridge as the keeping quality is not as good.

To understand why, we need to look at what makes food spoil and how the mechanisms work. There are two things we need to worry about: moulds and bacteria. To thrive, both of these need food, water and warmth. Cooling food in a fridge will slow the action of bacteria and freezing effectively stops their growth altogether. Jams and preserves, however, are made to store for a long time at room temperature.

Our first line of defence is to prevent entry of organisms that spoil our food. It really is important that the utensils and work surfaces are clean before we start. Surprisingly, one of the worst sources of bacteria in the kitchen is the dishcloth. That sits there, nice and damp with old bits of food at room temperature and is, therefore, the perfect growth medium for bacteria.

We soak ours overnight in a very dilute bleach solution and hang it over the tap to dry in the day when not in use. Not only does it look clean – and don't forget you cannot see bacteria without a microscope – but it is clean. Anti-bacterial liquid sprays are very cheap to buy and before starting food preparation it is worthwhile to wipe off all the surfaces with it using your clean dishcloth.

The next step is to ensure your utensils and pans are really clean. The jam pan may have been sitting there for months since it was last used and apart from dust, specks of the last batch of jam may have been left, happily growing bugs. Incidentally, when you've finished, it is worth making life easy for next time by thoroughly cleaning everything before you put it away.

Having burnt jam onto the bottom of a new pan (we all make mistakes!) one tip we found that worked was to add some biological washing powder to the pan, fill with water and bring to the boil. Left overnight, the burnt residue came off reasonably easily using some wire wool.

Never ignore the instructions in the method for sterilizing the jars, either. These should be clean and sparkly before you sterilize them and don't forget that the lids need to be suitable and require just as much attention to cleanliness. If you're making certain ketchups or sauces, always follow the secondary sterilization method covered on page 178.

The temperature of cooking jam, in excess of the boiling point of water, kills bacteria as well. With hygiene a 'belts and braces' approach is no bad thing.

Having kept the bugs out as far as we can, let's look at what stops the ones that get through from growing. Bacteria are single celled organisms that reproduce by dividing. In ideal conditions, they split into two every 20 minutes. One becomes two, two become four, four become eight and so on. In 24 hours one bacterium could theoretically have doubled 72 times to become 2,361,183,241,434,820,000,000 – that's an awful lot!

Don't panic. That's in ideal conditions and the conditions in our preserves are the opposite of ideal. Our main protection –

and what makes preserves work – is something called osmotic disruption. Just like the cells in our body, bacteria contain water and we suck that water out of the cell to kill them.

To see how this works, put a tablespoon of water on the worktop and pop a sugar cube in it. The water is sucked up into the cube. The sugar in jam works in just the same way: it sucks the water out of the bacteria, disrupting and killing it. Salt works in exactly the same way, hence its use as a food preservative.

Vinegar in chutneys has a similar effect, raising the acidity beyond the level in which the bugs can live. That's why it is critical to use vinegars with an acidity level above the 5 per cent minimum we mention in preserves.

Some natural substances like garlic juice and cayenne pepper also have antiseptic properties. Not only do they add flavour to your chutney, they help to prevent spoilage.

To sum it up, for successful and safe storage:
• Keep everything truly clean.
• Sterilize properly.
• Use the correct ingredients in the right proportions.

3

JAMS, JELLIES, MARMALADES, CURDS, BUTTERS AND CHEESES

Jams, jellies, marmalades, curds, butters and fruit cheeses are all popular ways of preserving summer fruits for use the year round. The cooking process does reduce the vitamin content, but much remains. In fact, jam was used as a way of staving off scurvy by early sailors when journeys took months, along with pickled cabbage and the limes that give the British the nickname of limey in some parts of the world. We assume they were eaten separately! The name jam, by the way, arises from the 'jamming' or bruising together of the fruit and sugar.

Jams are extremely versatile and have many uses. As well as accompanying bread and butter or toast, they can be used in homemade scones, pancakes, fillings for sponge cakes, biscuits, steamed puddings, baked puddings, trifles and ice-cream to name but a few.

Jams are a great way of preserving gluts of fruit. Not only can you use them straightaway, but you can freeze the fruit until you have enough for a jam making session.

Although freezing tends to destroy the texture of fruit, frozen fruit works perfectly well in a jam as the cooking process is going to break it down to some degree anyway and the mushiness caused by freezing doesn't matter. Incidentally, that's caused by the water in the fruit expanding as it freezes and breaking down the cell walls.

We grow our own strawberries and after eating them fresh we're often left with some over but not enough to be worthwhile turning into jam. We just prepare the strawberries (wash and remove the hard core) and then pop them into a sealed plastic bag and freeze them until we've enough for a jam making session. If you do use frozen fruit, increase the amount in the recipe by about 10 per cent to compensate for the loss of pectin caused by freezing.

If you've a decorative crab apple in the garden or perhaps your neighbours' gardens, then you can use up those crab apples in jams and jellies – they're a good source of pectin as well. Your neighbours might think those crab apples all over the lawn a nuisance but they'll change their minds when you give them a jar of crab apple jelly.

Don't forget that hedgerows are a great source of that quintessential British fruit, the blackberry. Blackberries and crab apples are a great mix. Whilst you are prowling the country lanes looking for blackberries, keep an eye out for self-seeded raspberries. We don't know why but wild free fruit jams always taste nicer!

Elderberries make a very traditional country jelly or mix well with blackberries. We were told as children, and you may have been told the same, that elderberries are poisonous. The truth is that unripe elderberries do contain tiny traces of cyanide and could cause vomiting and diarrhoea. So only pick ripe elderberries, which are plump and dark black in colour. Just take them in bunches. You can strip the berries off the twigs at home. Don't worry if a few unripe berries get through though, the cooking process makes them perfectly safe.

There are other wild berries you can use – hawthorn berries make a nice jelly when mixed with crab apples as do rowanberries (mountain ash). The crab apples provide the pectin needed for a good set.

You can make some unusual jams using vegetables. Carrot jam may not sound appealing but it tastes surprisingly pleasant and chilli jam is a revelation.

Equipment for Jam Making

The good news for those starting out making their own jam is that you can get away with using the equipment you're likely to have in your kitchen anyway. It's when you start making a lot that some specialist equipment really comes into its own.

Methylated Spirits

One item you may not have that is a must is a little bottle of methylated spirits for testing pectin. You can pick these up from any chemist.

Jars

The other 'must have' is, of course, a supply of jars. You can buy jars but we save up any jars that come into the house and ask our family and friends to save them up for us. The ideal jar will have held jam already and have the metal screw top that has a plastic coating. Technically you can use any jar or even glazed pot so long as it isn't chipped or cracked. You don't actually even need a lid as one can be improvised from cellophane and an elastic band. Unlike chutneys, an airtight seal is not absolutely necessary if a waxed disc is placed on the jam before the dust cover. Our experience though is that you are better off collecting the correct jars. As we said earlier, belt and braces is a good approach to hygiene in preserve making.

Always wash your jars thoroughly before putting them away until needed. This will make life easy for you when you start a jam making session as they'll only need a quick wash before sterilizing.

Preserving Pan

Although small quantities of jam can be made in a heavy-based saucepan or a pressure cooker without the lid, it is worth investing in a good quality, thick based, stainless steel preserving pan.

A good quality pan will cost a fair bit but does last a lifetime. Our preserving pan is now 25 years old and still going strong. It is stainless steel with a thick sandwiched aluminium core base and a ratchet system so the handle can be left up. Boiling jam gets very hot and keeping the handle up has saved us from carelessly getting severe burns more than once over the years.

Unlike saucepans, preserving pans are wider at the top than the base, which helps when reducing liquids as there is plenty of surface area to steam away excess liquid. Your jam pan is ideal for making chutney as well so it gets used more than you might think when you start out.

Wide Necked Funnel

Getting the hot jam into the jars can be a very messy business and a wide neck funnel will help no end. The alternative is to use a Pyrex type measuring jug but for the few pounds these funnels cost, they are worth buying. Ours is non-stick so cleaning up is easy!

Sugar Thermometer

A sugar thermometer is useful as a guide to knowing if the setting point has been reached although we still test using a saucer as described in the methods. We managed for years without one, but once again, it only costs a couple of pounds to buy. Such thermometers usually read from 10–204° Celsius. Ordinary room thermometers cannot be used.

Waxed Paper Circles

Immediately after the jars are filled they should be wiped clean and a waxed paper circle with the waxed side down put on the top of the jam before the lid is screwed on. The waxed paper circle should be absolutely flat on the surface of the jam to prevent mould from developing. You can get away without them if using plastic coated lids on the jars, but an additional line of defence against spoilage is useful.

Labels

You need to label the jars with the contents and date. You can buy labels to write on with decorative borders or just buy a sheet of labels for use in a computer very cheaply. If you give away your jam as a gift, a nice label makes all the difference.

Stone Remover

If you make cherry jam, then a stone remover will save you hours. There is nothing worse than breaking a tooth on an unexpected stone in a jar of jam.

Jelly Bag

For jellies and cheeses you will need a straining bag. We picked up a strainer set which includes a frame that holds the bag above a bowl, allowing you to concentrate on pouring the contents in but, as you'll see on page 76, you can make one yourself.

Other Items

The following items will probably be in your kitchen anyway.

A long handled wooden spoon for stirring your jam and a slotted metal spoon for removing stones and scum from jams.

A decent set of scales. It's a recipe for disaster guessing at weight when jam making and every cook needs a good set of scales anyway.

A colander is useful for draining and a metal sieve is needed when making jellies and jams.

A grater or a mandolin is useful for marmalade as is a zester, and a peeler comes in handy as well.

A Pyrex or similar heat resistant measuring jug is useful.

Muslin is needed for straining and wrapping spices, etc.

All of the above can be found in good cookshops or online shops.

Jam Making Method

General Preparation

Before you start, check you have everything you need. Not that we've ever gone to the cupboard and discovered that we'd used that bag of sugar we would have sworn was there!

Clear the decks for action. You're going to have a large pan full of very hot, above the boiling point of water hot, jam as well as jars sterilizing, scales weighing and fruit being prepared. Got something in the sink? Wash it up and put it away before it's in your way. A clear working area will make the whole process easier and, most importantly, safer.

When you've cleared up ready to start, wipe down with an anti-bacterial spray. Cleanliness is vital in any food production and it only takes a minute now the surfaces are clear.

Next get out the jars and lids and give them a wash. Leave upside down to drain off and dry before you are busy stirring the jam and ready to sterilize them. Always get a couple of extra jars out as well. You may end up with a little more jam than the recipe suggested and it's a lot easier if you're prepared for it.

Now we're ready to make our jam.

Select and Prepare the Fruit

To some degree the quality of your jam depends on the fruit. Having said that, you can make excellent jams with substandard fruits. Misshapen fruits or damaged fruit are fine to use, the shape will not be particularly relevant when they've been cooked. Cut off any damaged bits, remove stems, stones, etc, and then rinse off, draining well.

With wild or home grown blackberries, raspberries, etc, soak for ten minutes in a large bowl of water. You'll be surprised how many little maggots and other bugs float to the top where you can skim them out. It may not be pleasant, but it's better than incorporating them into your jam. Commercially purchased berries rarely suffer from these guests but they've been sprayed with pesticides. You can't see pesticide residue.

Under ripe fruits may be hard even when cooked into jam but over ripe fruits are generally fine. One thing to watch for is that over ripe fruit tends to contain less pectin and you may need to add more pectin than normal to get a set if there is a high proportion of over ripe fruit.

Weigh and Start Cooking

Weigh your prepared fruit next. Although a recipe may call for 2 kg of fruit and 2 kg of sugar, it's the ratio that's important. In other words, if you only have 1.5 kg of fruit, then you reduce the amount of sugar to match. Remember, recipes are a guide and you will adapt them to suit your needs and taste.

Some fruits have a higher water content than others and therefore require more water when cooking to soften and extract the juice from the fruit. Especially with fruits that need little or no water, start cooking slowly on a lower heat until the juices have come out. This helps to prevent the fruit sticking and burning on the base of the pan.

A Rough Guide to How Much Water to Use

The individual recipes here will tell you how much water to use but when you start adapting the recipes or creating your own, these guidelines should help you judge. If you do not have enough water, the fruit may end up with tough skins and not release enough pectin for a good set. Too much water can be evaporated off by boiling but over-boiling the jam will impair the flavour and colour.

Fruits that need very little water (just enough to prevent burning on the pan base) or none at all include the juicy berries, strawberries, raspberries, elderberries, etc.

Stiff textured fruits, such as plums, greengages, rhubarb and apples, will need about half the volume of the fruit added as water.

Tough skinned fruit like blackcurrants and hard textured fruits such as quinces, medlars and pears need about an equal volume of water to fruit.

For the citrus fruits – oranges, lemons, grapefruit and limes – you need between twice and three times the volume of fruit as water.

Acid

To set properly, your jam needs the correct proportions of acid, pectin and sugar. Acid also affects the colour of the final jam, making it brighter and cuts the sweetness so the jam tastes more of the fruit than sugar. Some fruits are naturally high in acid but others are low so we need to compensate for this by adding acid **at the start before we begin cooking**.

The recipes will tell you how much acid you need to add, usually in the form of lemon juice. Incidentally, when squeezing a lemon you will get more juice out if the lemon is warm. Ten seconds in a microwave or popping the lemon in a bowl of hot water for a couple of minutes will enable you to extract all the juice.

Of course, you may find it more convenient to keep a bottle of lemon juice in the cupboard. Two tablespoons of lemon juice is the equivalent to the juice of one lemon.

You can substitute for lemon juice by dissolving one level teaspoon of tartaric acid or citric acid powder in half a teacup of water for each lemon. Personally we prefer to stick to lemons rather than adding chemical powders like a food technician.

However, instead of lemon juice you can add the equivalent of one lemon with 140 ml (¼ pint) gooseberry or redcurrant juice. Your choice will affect the final flavour but don't omit the acid.

If you're developing your own recipe, you can judge the acidity of your fruit by comparing the taste with that of a tablespoon of lemon juice in half a cup of water. If the fruit tastes sweeter than your dilute lemon juice, you need to add acid. It can be difficult to judge at first but like many skills you get better with practice.

Fruits Generally Containing Adequate Acid	Fruits Generally Lacking in Acid
Cooking apples	Bilberries
Early blackberries	Late Blackberries
Blackcurrants	Blueberries
Cranberries	Sweet cherries
Damsons	Strawberries
Gooseberries	Peaches
Loganberries	Pears
Plums	Quinces
Raspberries	Medlars
Redcurrants	
Morello cherries	

Cooking the Fruit

Start cooking on a very low heat, especially where you are not using additional water, to avoid burning on the base of the pan. Once the juices are running you can turn the heat up to medium and bring it to the boil. It's important to keep stirring occasionally or the fruit will stick.

Once it's boiling, turn the heat down to just a simmer. We're cooking the fruit to soften the skin and flesh and evaporate excess water to concentrate the fruit pulp. At the same time we're extracting the pectin from the fruit, which is vital for a good set.

How long to simmer is a matter of judgement. Soft fruits like strawberries may be ready in just 15 minutes but stiffer fruits like plums can take 30 minutes and fruits like black-currants with hard skins can take 45 minutes.

It's vital to taste before deciding it is ready. 'Does it really have a good strong fruit flavour and are the skins soft?' is the question to ask yourself. If you add the sugar before the fruit is properly cooked, no amount of boiling will soften hard skins.

If you've used wet fruit or too much water, you may need to extend the simmering time to evaporate excess water. A good strong pulp makes the best tasting jam.

You can use a pressure cooker to decrease the cooking time but we have found this unsatisfactory. You have less control over timing as you cannot open a pressure cooker midway through cooking and so over cooking can easily take place. The pressure cooker does not evaporate excess water like an open pan so normal boiling is often still required and, in addition, we felt it impaired the final flavour.

Pectin

Pectin is what is known as a gelling agent. In other words, it causes things to gel or our jam to set. It occurs naturally in some fruits and is absent in others so we need to keep that in mind when making our jams and add as necessary.

Some recipes balance a fruit high in pectin with one low in pectin to ensure a set, such as Blackberry and Apple Jam. The high pectin content in the apples compensates for the low pectin content in the blackberries.

If you are making a jam with low pectin fruits that also require acid, you can use freshly squeezed lemon juice for the acid and then cut the lemon peel into chunks and boil them with the fruit in a muslin bag. The pith of citrus fruits is high in pectin and the boiling releases it into the jam. Remove the bag when you've finished boiling. Do be aware that the pith of citrus fruits tends to be very bitter and can impart this to the final flavour of jams and marmalades.

You can buy pectin for domestic jam making in the shops. It comes either as a liquid in a bottle or a powder in sachets. Generally instructions for use are given on the packet or bottle. If, for example, the instructions on Silver Spoon powdered pectin say 'use 13g of pectin powder per kilogram of sugar' but you know your jam is only slightly deficient in pectin, then you can halve the amount to prevent the jam being too solidly set.

We always keep some pectin powder in the cupboard. There is a 'best before' date on it but it's in sealed airtight foil sachets and in our experience doesn't deteriorate, even two years past that date, so long as left in the sachets. We wouldn't be so confident in exceeding the shelf life to that degree with liquid pectin though.

Liquid pectin, usually under the Certo brand name, also has a drawback that once opened it needs to be kept in the refrigerator and used within a week. Being a dilute solution of pectin and sugars from apples, it is an ideal medium for yeasts and moulds that could destroy the pectin and turn the sugar into alcohol. There is enough preservative to stop this happening immediately, but only if it is kept refrigerated and used quickly.

Unlike the pectin naturally in the fruit, the commercial pectin is added later in the process. Powdered pectin is usually added with the sugar and liquid pectin towards the end of the process after the sugar has been boiled.

You can also buy jam sugar that contains added pectin. Do not confuse this with preserving sugar (see Adding the Sugar on page 31).

Homemade Pectin Stock

You can make your own pectin stock if you wish from either apples or citrus fruits. Since the citrus pectin stock is somewhat bitter and more expensive to make, whereas apple stock is cheaper and a better flavour, we stick with apple stock.

Take about 1.8 kg (4 lb) of washed cooking apples or crab apples. Slice and place in a stainless steel or enamel saucepan. Don't peel or bother coring, removing the pips, etc. Just cover with water and bring to the boil. Simmer until the apples are mushy and then strain through a metal sieve, pushing much of the pulp through into another pot.

Leave this overnight and the next day bring back to the boil and reduce the liquid by half. You can get an idea of the strength of the resulting stock by testing as described on the next page. Further reduction by simmering will increase the strength.

Your homemade stock will keep for a couple of days in the fridge. You can freeze it but freezing reduces the pectin content. You can also bottle your stock for storage.

Take a sterilized Kilner jar and place it in a pot of boiling water with a trivet underneath (or the heat will crack the jar). Pour the stock into the jar and boil for 5 minutes before sealing airtight.

As a rule, use about 285 ml (½ pint) of your stock per 1.8 kg (4 lb) of fruit very low in pectin like strawberries, less with medium pectin fruits (see chart below).

Fruits Rich in Pectin	Fruits with Medium Pectin	Fruits Lacking in Pectin
Cooking apples Crab apples Blackcurrants Cranberries Damsons Plums Redcurrants Quince	Apricots Greengages Loganberries Raspberries Blackberries (early)	Blackberries (late) Cherries Elderberries Peaches Pears Rhubarb Strawberries

Testing for Pectin

This really is crucial when making your jam, not only do different fruits have different amounts of pectin but it can vary according to season or ripeness of the fruit. **The only way to know if you have enough pectin for a good set is to test for it**. However, if you add too much pectin your jam will be pretty solid, so it comes down to judgement as well as recipes. We're dealing with natural fruits, not production line products!

There is a proven standard test for pectin content and luckily it's hard to go wrong with.

Take one teaspoon of clear fruit juice and drop into a cold glass or cup, allow it to cool for a minute and then add three teaspoons of methylated spirit and stir around or gently shake.

If a large clot forms from the juice, adequate pectin for a good set has been extracted and the sugar may be added.

If there is only a medium amount of pectin, several small clots will form. It is probably going to be worth adding some additional pectin to ensure a good set. With experience you will be able to judge how lacking it is and balance the addition of pectin accordingly.

If there is very little pectin content it will break into small pieces and additional pectin will definitely have to be added.

If you think the fruit you are using should be adequate in pectin but the test says otherwise, then try simmering for another 5 or 10 minutes and re-test. It may be that you have just not extracted enough pectin from the fruit and this will sort the problem.

Adding Pectin

If after further boiling your test shows that your fruit is still lacking in pectin you can add homemade stock and re-test. If you are using commercial pectin powder, add this with the sugar; if using liquid commercial pectin, add after the sugar has boiled.

Adding the Sugar
Types of Sugar

Although you can, in theory at least, make jams using honey, molasses and even maple syrup we'll stick with sugar and leave those for the adventurous. You can use brown sugar or unrefined sugar but there is really no point unless you're developing a recipe and need it for flavour.

For all jams we would use ordinary cheap granulated sugar. Most often you will find it cheapest in kilogram bags as it's a supermarket loss leader but we have occasionally found 2 and 4 kilo bags even cheaper. Just go for the cheapest you can find. Ignore any nonsense you may hear about cane sugar being best or even caster sugar!

You can buy preserving sugar which has larger crystals and is supposedly better for using with high pectin fruits, being less prone to burning and producing less scum. Stirring will prevent burning and we'll deal with the scum later anyway, so it's not a product we bother with.

Jam sugar is granulated sugar with added pectin. Don't confuse it with preserving sugar. Some people think you always need to use special jam sugar (as well as pectin) and wonder why their jam is so well set it is hard to cut with a knife. It is, however, a convenient way to add pectin to some jams where the fruit or vegetable has none. Where a recipe calls for jam sugar, we would tend to use ordinary sugar with pectin powder or stock being added. If you're just starting out, then jam sugar is simpler, especially if you change the quantities in your recipe.

Warming the Sugar

As you come towards the end of simmering your fruit, weigh out your sugar and put it into an oven dish in a low oven for five minutes or so. Although not strictly necessary, warming the sugar helps it to dissolve faster and avoids the risk of the sugar crystallizing in the jam later, especially when acid and pectin are high. The fruit will return to the boil faster as well since you've already put some heat into the sugar.

Whether warmed or not, add the sugar fairly slowly stirring well and dissolving it all before adding more.

Amount of Sugar

Most recipes for fruit with a moderate amount of pectin call for an equal amount of sugar to fruit. However, in theory, the best setting and keeping qualities are obtained with a jam containing 60 per cent of sugar and fruit which is high in pectin; for example, gooseberries and blackcurrants can have up to 1½ times volume of sugar to fruit. Personally, we've never found any problem in setting or storing high pectin fruit jams and no improvement to the flavour by adding the extra sugar so we only use the 50/50 combination. However, when using a fruit that is low in pectin (such as cherries), it is advisable to increase the proportion of fruit to sugar to allow more pectin to be extracted. The same applies when using frozen fruit: allow 10 per cent more fruit to sugar to compensate for the loss of pectin caused by freezing. Alternatively, add more pectin stock or powder.

The Fast Boil

Having got the sugar all dissolved, the next step is to bring it to a fast boil. Unlike water that boils at 100° Celsius, jam with its sugar boils at about 105° Celsius. This is when it has reached the setting point where the action of boiling has caused a chemical reaction in your jam.

You want to take the jam up to temperature as quickly as possible so turn the heat up as high as it will go. You will need to keep stirring occasionally to avoid burning onto the pan base which brings us to a safety point.

Use a long handled spoon for stirring. We found a wooden one cheaply. If you get a splash of jam onto yourself, often when a bubble bursts on the surface, it will scald you. Remember it is likely to be above the boiling point of water and, worse still, it is sticky and thick. A drop of boiling jam will hold its heat longer than water and you can get some quite nasty scalds. Be careful.

You can usually tell when it has reached a fast boil as it continues to bubble even when stirred. This usually means the setting point has been reached.

If you have a sugar thermometer, you can check the temperature. Dip the sugar thermometer in hot water to avoid thermal shock when it goes into the jam, stir the jam, then immerse the thermometer into it. Do not allow the bulb to touch the bottom of the pan as it may break from the temperature of the base of the pan. It will also read wrongly as the temperature by the heat source is higher than the average of the pan. If the temperature is around 105° Celsius (220° Fahrenheit), setting point has probably been reached. Sugar thermometers are a good guide but not 100 per cent – and we managed for many years without one.

Another indicator test that the jam is ready is to dip your wooden spoon into the jam, remove it, and after a second or two tilt the spoon so that the jam drips. If the jam is almost set and the drops run together in large flakes, setting point has been reached.

Setting Test

When you think the jam has reached the setting point, it's time for the final test. Turn the heat down – you don't want to over-boil – and then put 1 teaspoon of jam onto a cold saucer and allow to cool for a minute. Tip: pop the saucer into the fridge for ten minutes first so it's quite cold. Push the surface of the jam gently with your fingertip and, if the surface wrinkles, setting point is reached.

If it doesn't set, bring back to a fast boil for a minute or two and re-test.

Fig. 2. Place a spoonful of hot jam on a cold plate (from the fridge), allow it to thicken for half a minute, then push with your fingertip. If, as shown, the surface wrinkles, the jam can be potted.

Cleaning the Jam

You'll notice that there is some bubbly sugar scum rising to the surface of your jam. Leave the pan on the cooker with the heat turned off for ten to fifteen minutes to allow all the scum to rise to the surface and then skim it off with a slotted spoon. There will be some left but we can sort that out easily by adding a knob of butter to the pan and gently stirring it in. If all has gone well we're now ready to pot up into sterilized jars.

You can use a few drops of glycerine instead of the butter, but we prefer to keep our ingredients as natural as possible.

Sterilizing the Jars

Although the sugar in your jam will protect against bacteria growing, it won't stop moulds from developing so it really is critical to sterilize your jars. Please don't just wash them and think it will be all right – it won't. We often get emails from people asking why their jam has gone mouldy when the shop bought jam doesn't. The answer is simple: hygiene and sterilization.

As we said earlier, your jars should be washed clean and shiny before you start but this is not sterile. You've just got the thick off, as we say.

The easiest way to sterilize your jars is to place them upright on a baking sheet with the lids beside them in a very low oven for ten minutes or so. A good time to do this is when you warm your sugar. After you take the sugar out, close the oven door and switch it off. The residual heat will keep the jars sterile until use.

You can use a microwave to sterilize jam jars although it is a lot more fuss than the oven method and will not cope with more than a few jars at a time. Quarter fill the jar with cold water, dip in your fingers and rub your dampened fingers completely around the jar. If the jar has a lid, shake the water around with the lid on but don't leave it on when you put it into the microwave. Metal items in microwaves cause them to spark and can destroy the microwave.

Microwave the jar for one minute on full power. Everywhere the moisture has touched will be brought to boiling point and sterilized. Pour out the water, **taking care because the jar will be hot**, and use for your jam.

The third method of sterilizing jars is to put them in a pan with a trivet in the base of the pan and boil for a few minutes. The trivet stops the jars from cracking due to direct heat conduction.

Once again, it's a lot of fuss compared with the oven method. With both the microwave and boiling methods you need to drain the jars thoroughly before filling. You can also sterilize your jars in a dishwasher using a hot wash but this is very energy inefficient.

Potting Up

We should now be ready to fill our jars with the jam. When you are using whole fruits like strawberries and with marmalades with the peel in, there's a tendency for these to float to the top. If you allow the jam to cool a little, just to the point where there is a skin forming on the top, then stirring gently before potting up will help avoid this.

The easiest way to fill your jars is to use a wide necked funnel in the jar and a Pyrex jug or large ladle for transferring from pan to funnel.

Once again, be careful. Even at this stage your jam is pretty hot.

Fill the jar as near to the top as you can. As it cools, it will shrink a little, dropping a quarter inch or so below the rim.

Once filled, put a waxed paper circle (wax side down) onto the surface of the jam and then put your lid on. As the jam cools and contracts, it will pull the lid on very firmly, improving and making the seal airtight.

Although lids are not strictly necessary, the chances of mould getting in spoiling your jam over the coming months are virtually zero using a lid. We've never had a problem with mould using this method over many years.

Leave the jars, which will be quite hot from the contents, on a heatproof mat to cool down. If you've made your jam in the afternoon, leaving overnight is best. There is always a temptation to check the set and taste but don't open your jars until you are ready to use the jam. Otherwise you undo all your good works sterilizing the jars.

Even if the recipe indicates you will make 2.3 kg (5 lb) of jam, because of variations in moisture content and so forth, it is never exact. We have a few small jars which we use to pot up the inevitable remainder. There's always a little jam left over and if it isn't worth potting up, we put it in a small dish in the fridge. This cools it quickly and you can set your mind at rest regarding the set and taste the jam almost immediately.

Clean and Label

When the jars have cooled down and the jam has set, clean off any spills. This isn't just cosmetic – spills will grow mouldy and that will not exactly make your jam appetizing. Plus when you eventually open the jar, there will be mould spores around.

If you want to add a little sparkle, use a dab of methylated spirits on a paper towel to polish the jars up. Label with the date and you're done. You've made your jam.

Store in a cool dark place for the longest life. Most fruit jams, stored correctly, will easily keep for 12 months. We have had jams stored for a lot longer that were perfectly good. If you are going to take more than a couple of weeks to eat an opened jar of jam, or in warm weather, store in the refrigerator.

Low Sugar, Microwave and Machine Made Jams

Low Sugar Jams

You can actually make jams with lower than the usual 50 or 60 per cent sugar content. Although we can understand people being concerned about high sugar intake in modern diets, most of that tends to be in processed foods. Normal sugar jam, in moderation, is fine. It's too much of what you fancy that does you harm.

As a rule the proportion of sugar to fruit in low sugar jam is 1.5 to 2.0, so they still contain a fair amount of sugar. However, setting is often a problem unless there is ample pectin and acid in the final boiling and even then the set will be less firm than usual.

The jam will keep for only a few weeks unless stored in airtight jars and, once opened, will remain in good condition for only 10 to 14 days.

Diabetic jams using sugar substitute and pectin are a separate thing altogether and really are not within the scope of this book.

Microwave Jams

You can make small amounts of jam in a microwave, but since most conventional recipes only make about half a dozen jars we don't do it ourselves.

You must use a large bowl, as large as will fit into the chamber for jam making. At a minimum it needs to be twice as large and preferably three times as large as the final jam volume. It is important to remember that when you add the sugar to the boiled fruit, the bulk will double.

Cook the fruit on full power for around 4 minutes until it is soft.

Stir in the sugar until it has dissolved and then cook again on high power for 3 minutes, before stirring thoroughly.

Continue to do this until the jam has cooked for about 18 minutes, or until the jam sets when a little is placed on a chilled saucer.

Stir in a small knob of butter or a few drops of glycerine to get rid of any scum.

Leave to stand for 5 minutes and then pour into hot sterilized jars and seal.

NB Never use a sugar thermometer in a microwave!

Jam Making Machines

Nowadays domestic jam making machines are available. Like bread making machines, they tend to produce a pretty good result so long as you follow the recipes to the letter and are looking to make smaller quantities. Some bread making machines also have a jam making function.

Personally we prefer the traditional methods if only because they allow experimentation and alteration of the recipes and are more controllable.

When Things Go Wrong

Poor Set

The most common problem with jam is the set. Despite having done things by the book and having been sure it passed the saucer setting test, the next morning you realize the jam is far too sloppy.

Don't despair. You can usually rescue things with a bit of extra work. The two most common reasons for the jam not setting are it not having been heated to the setting point properly or lack of pectin.

Get the equipment out and pour the jam back into the pan. Try re-boiling for a minute, stirring continually to prevent sticking and then re-test. If this doesn't work, add some pectin. About half the amount you would originally have used should be enough. The commercial pectin, either bottled or powder, is the easiest for this. Re-test and you should be all right.

Watch out for over compensating or you can end up with a jam so firm you have trouble getting the spoon into it.

Do remember to wash and re-sterilize the jars before re-potting. Discard the old waxed paper circles and use fresh.

Mould Develops in Store

There's no cure for this: discard the jam. Next time you make jam pay special attention to hygiene, sterilizing the jars, etc, and use airtight lids fitted whilst the jam is hot. Avoid storing in damp places as this encourages mould and there will be more microscopic spores floating around.

Fruit Floated to the Top

This seems to happen quite often with strawberry jam. The trick is to let the jam cool in the pan until a skin starts to form on the surface. Then stir to re-distribute the fruit before potting up.

Burnt Flavour

Keep stirring when bringing to the boil to avoid things sticking and burning. Label the jam as 'Burnt Strawberry' and everyone will think you're a genius!

Fermentation

Small bubbles start to appear in the jam. Basically yeast has got in and is starting to make alcohol from the sugar. It is a hygiene problem. You can try re-boiling and re-potting, taking extra care over sterilizing the jars, etc. It may impair the flavour but it's worth a try to rescue the batch.

Sugar Crystals in the Jam

This is thankfully not too common. There is no cure for it but the jam is perfectly edible anyway. It's usually caused by over-boiling past the setting point or adding too much sugar. Insufficient acid is another cause.

Strawberry Jam (1)

Makes about 2.7 kg (6 lb)

This jam works better with smallish, slightly under-ripe berries as they have more pectin. It is also a good jam to make with frozen strawberries as they tend to mush down anyway. If you do use frozen berries, allow an extra 10 per cent of fruit to compensate for the pectin lost during freezing.

1.8 kg (4 lb) strawberries
Juice of 2 lemons or equivalent
1.8 kg (4 lb) sugar

Hull (remove the hard core) the strawberries, wash and drain well.

Put into a preserving pan with the lemon juice.

Simmer gently until the fruit is soft.

Test for pectin (see page 30).

Remove from the hob, add the sugar, stirring until it has dissolved.

Return to the heat, bring to the boil and boil rapidly for 5–10 minutes until setting point is reached.

Remove the scum and leave to cool for about 10 minutes. Stir before transferring to the jars as this helps the fruit to be evenly distributed and stops it rising.

Pot and seal while still warm. Label when cool.

Strawberry Jam (2)

Makes about 2.7 kg (6 lb)

For a strawberry jam with whole strawberries, you'll need to add pectin stock as extracting enough pectin for a set breaks the fruit down. Instead of pectin stock you can make this easily using jam sugar.

1.8 kg (4 lb) small, whole strawberries
1.8 kg (4 lb) sugar
Juice of 2 lemons or equivalent
200 ml (7 fl oz) pectin stock (see page 29)

Hull the strawberries, wash and drain well.

Put into a preserving pan with the sugar and lemon juice.

Heat gently until the sugar has dissolved, then bring to the boil and simmer for about 5 minutes.

Remove from the heat and stir in the pectin stock.

Cool for about 10 minutes, then stir again to distribute the fruit evenly.

Pot and seal whilst still warm. Label when cool.

Plum Jam

Makes about 2.7 kg (6 lb)

Plum jam is very easy to make as plums have a lot of pectin naturally so setting is never a problem. For a more distinctive taste, crack open about 6 of the stones and remove the kernels and put the kernels in with the fruit and water.

**1.8 kg (4 lb) plums (after the stones have been
    removed)**
570 ml (1 pint) water
1.8 kg (4 lb) sugar

Wash and wipe the plums. Cut into halves and remove the stones.

Put into a pan with the water and simmer gently until the fruit is soft.

Test for pectin (see page 30).

Remove from the heat, add the sugar, stirring until the sugar has dissolved.

Return to the hob, bring to the boil and boil rapidly until setting point is reached.

Remove the scum. Pot and seal whilst still hot. Label when cool.

Damson Jam

Makes about 2.7 kg (6 lb)

A very easy jam to make as damsons have loads of pectin. With their strong flavour, it's not necessary to use more than the 1.8 kg/4 lb of fruit even taking into account the weight of the stones.

1.8 kg (4 lb) damsons
140 ml (¼ pint) water
1.8 kg (4 lb) sugar

Wash and wipe the damsons. Pick over to remove stalks.

Put into a pan with the water and simmer gently until the fruit is soft, occasionally pressing the damsons against the sides of the pan to break open and release the stones.

Remove the stones.

Test for pectin (see page 30).

Remove from the heat, add the sugar, stirring until it has dissolved.

Return to the hob, bring to the boil and boil rapidly for about 10 minutes until the jam sets when tested.

Remove the remainder of the stones as they rise to the surface.

Remove the scum. Pot and seal while still hot. Label when cool.

Cherry Jam

Makes about 2.3 kg (5 lb)

Usually cherry jam is made with morello cherries, which have a reasonable amount of pectin. Ripe dessert (sweet) cherries are low in pectin and it can be difficult to get a good set. If, when testing for pectin, it is insufficient, add 150 ml (5 fl oz) of pectin stock along with the sugar. Using less sugar to fruit for this jam allows more pectin to be extracted.

1.8 kg (4 lb) cherries (weight after stones have been removed)
Juice of 2 lemons
1.4 kg (3 lb) sugar

Wash the cherries and remove the stones.

Put into a pan with the lemon juice and simmer gently until the fruit is soft.

Test for pectin (see page 30).

Remove from the heat, add the sugar, stirring until it has dissolved.

Return to the hob, bring to the boil and boil rapidly for about 10 minutes until the jam sets when tested.

Remove the scum. Pot and seal whilst still hot. Label when cool.

Blackberry and Apple Jam

Makes about 2.7 kg (6 lb)

Ripe blackberries are lacking in pectin and you would have problems in getting a good set without the addition of the apples. You can also add some lemon juice to taste as they are also lacking in acid.

Instead of cooking apples, you can use crab apples which are also very high in pectin. Apples tend to carry the other fruit flavour and are neutral in the jam.

450 g (1 lb) cooking apples (after peeling and removing the core)
1.4 kg (3 lb) blackberries
140 ml (¼ pint) water
1.8 kg (4 lb) sugar

Peel and core the apples. Weigh and cut into slices. Put into a preserving pan with just enough water to prevent the apples burning.

Simmer gently until the apples are soft.

Pick over and wash the blackberries, drain well and put into a pan with 140 ml (¼ pint) water. Simmer until tender and add to the cooked apples.

Test for pectin (see page 30).

Remove from the heat, add the sugar and stir until dissolved.

Return to the hob, bring to the boil and boil rapidly for about 10 minutes, until the jam sets when tested.

Remove the scum. Pot and seal whilst still hot. Label when cool.

Raspberry Jam

Makes about 2.7 kg (6 lb)

Raspberries generally contain enough pectin for a good set so if they fail the pectin test, simmering for a few minutes more usually does the trick.

1.8 kg (4 lb) raspberries
1.8 kg (4 lb) sugar

Wash the raspberries if necessary and drain well.

Put into a preserving pan.

Simmer until some juice has been extracted.

Test for pectin (see page 30).

Add the sugar, stirring until it has dissolved.

Bring to the boil and boil rapidly for 5–10 minutes until the jam sets when tested.

Remove the scum and leave to cool slightly so that the fruit will not rise in the jars.

Pot and seal while still warm. Label when cool.

Gooseberry Jam

Makes about 2.7 kg (6 lb)

Gooseberries are full of pectin and acidic in their own right, so this is really easy to make. Traditional recipes call for a higher proportion of sugar, 1½ times sugar to the volume of fruit, but we have found this unnecessary.

Gooseberry jams tend to go pinkish in cooking. If you want a green coloured jam, choose a green variety that retains it colour when cooked and make sure the fruit is slightly under-ripe.

1.8 kg (4 lb) gooseberries
1.1 litres (2 pints) water
1.8 kg (4 lb) sugar

Top and tail the gooseberries. Wash well and drain.

Put into a pan with the water and simmer gently until soft.

Test for pectin (see page 30).

Remove from the heat, add the sugar, stirring until the sugar has dissolved.

Return to the hob, bring to the boil and boil rapidly for about 5 minutes until the jam sets when tested.

Remove the scum.

Pot and seal while still hot. Label when cool.

Blackcurrant Jam

Makes about 2.7 kg (6 lb)

This is another jam that traditional recipes call for a higher proportion of sugar, 1½ times sugar to the volume of fruit. We've tried it both ways and have found no real advantage to the extra sugar. Feel free to try it both ways to see if you can tell the difference.

1.8 kg (4 lb) blackcurrants
1.1 litres (2 pints) water
1.8 kg (4 lb) sugar

Remove the stalks from the currants, then wash and drain carefully.

Put into the pan with the water, bring to the boil, then simmer until the fruit is soft and pulpy and the contents of the pan are reduced by about a third. Take care not to cook the fruit too quickly or the skins will toughen. You'll need to stir frequently whilst the pulp is reducing to prevent sticking.

Test for pectin (see page 30).

Remove from the heat, add the sugar, stirring until the sugar has dissolved.

Return to the hob, bring to the boil and boil rapidly until the jam sets when tested.

Remove the scum.

Pot and seal while still hot. Label when cool.

Rhubarb and Orange Jam

Makes about 2.7 kg (6 lb)

This is an unusual jam, oranges being more associated with marmalade, but it works really well. The additional lemon zest and the orange rind makes it more like a marmalade as well. The set is different from 'normal', closer to a conserve.

1.4 kg (3 lb) rhubarb
1.4 kg (3 lb) sugar
Grated rind and juice of 1 lemon
2 thin-skinned oranges

Chop the rhubarb into 2.5 cm (1 inch) lengths.

Put alternate layers of rhubarb and sugar in a bowl. Add the lemon rind and juice. Cover and leave overnight.

Boil the oranges whole in water for about 1 hour.

Cut the oranges into small pieces, discarding any pips, and add to the rhubarb. Stir well.

Place in a pan, bring slowly to the boil, stirring until the sugar has dissolved.

Boil rapidly until setting point is reached.

Remove the scum and leave to cool slightly. Pot into warm sterilized jars and seal whilst still warm. Label when cool.

Marrow and Ginger Jam

Makes about 2.7 kg (6 lb)

For an extra kick put 3 or 4 chillies in the muslin with the ginger. This makes a great breakfast jam, which certainly wakes your taste buds up.

1.4 kg (3 lb) marrow
450 g (1 lb) dessert or cooking apples
Juice of 2 lemons
56 g (2 oz) root ginger
1.8 kg (4 lb) sugar
5 fl oz (140 ml) pectin stock (see page 29)

Peel the marrow, discard the seeds and cut into cubes.

Peel and core the apples and cut the flesh into cubes.

Place the marrow and apple in a pan, steam until tender and then mash.

Add the lemon juice.

Bruise the root ginger and wrap in a piece of muslin and place in the pan.

Bring back to simmering point, then remove from the heat and stir in the sugar until it has dissolved.

Bring to the boil and boil for about 20 minutes, stirring occasionally as the pulp thickens.

Stir in the pectin stock towards the end.

Remove the muslin bag and pot into hot sterilized jars and cover. Label when cool.

Chilli Jam

Makes about 1.4 kg (3 lb)

You can do the same with green peppers and chillies but use white wine or cider vinegar. Do be aware that chilli peppers vary greatly in hotness. If you are using a habenero then you might like to reduce their number. Also take care not to touch your eyes after handling the chillies.

It's surprising how the initial sweetness is gradually overtaken as the heat comes through. It's wonderful on a sharp Cheddar cheese sandwich as a pickle and also makes a good accompaniment to a curry.

4 or 5 large red peppers (about 900g (2 lb) in weight)
As many red chillies as you want – about 20
855 ml (1½ pints) red wine vinegar
sugar – preferably caster
6 or 7 more red chillies
pectin stock

Quarter the peppers, remove the core but leave the pith in, and chop into small chunks.

Put the chillies (you can halve them if they don't fit) through a blender until finely chopped. You may need to do this in several batches.

Put the chilli/pepper mix into a preserving pan and stir in the vinegar.

Bring to the boil and then reduce to a simmer for about 20 minutes.

Push the mixture through a fine sieve and discard the pulp. Measure the purée and for each 570 ml (1 pint) allow 1.4 kg (3 lb) of sugar and 285 ml (½ pint) pectin stock.

Put the purée back into a preserving pan and re-heat to a simmer.

Remove from the heat and stir in the sugar until it has dissolved.

Finely chop another 6 or 7 chillies (take the tops off but you can leave the seeds in so it's easier to do in a blender) and stir these into the pan.

Return to the heat and bring to a boil. Boil rapidly for 1 or 2 minutes and then stir in the pectin stock.

Allow to cool slightly and then pot into hot, sterilized jars and seal. Label when cool.

Fresh Apricot Jam

Makes about 3.2 kg (7 lb)

For a variation, stir in 7 tablespoons of brandy or apricot brandy at the end before potting.

1.8 kg (4 lb) fresh apricots (weight after stones have been removed
430 ml (¾ pint) water
1.8 kg (4 lb) sugar

Wash and drain the apricots. Cut in half and remove the stones.

Crack a few of the stones and tie the kernels in a piece of muslin.

Put the apricots, kernels and water into a pan and simmer the fruit until it is tender and the contents of the pan have reduced by about a third.

Take out the kernels and test for pectin (see page 30). If low, add 4 tablespoons of lemon juice.

Stir in the sugar until it is dissolved.

Return to the heat and bring to the boil. Boil rapidly for about 10 minutes until the jam sets when tested.

Remove any scum. Pot and seal.

Label when cool.

Dried Apricot Jam

Makes about 4.5 kg (10 lb)

For a variation, stir in 112 g (4 oz) of blanched shredded almonds with the sugar.

900 g (2 lb) dried apricots
3.4 litres (6 pints) water
2 tablespoons lemon juice
2.7 kg (6 lb) sugar

Cut the apricots into quarters. Place them in a large bowl with the water, making sure that they are completely covered, and leave to soak for about 24 hours.

Transfer to a pan, with the water, and add 2 tablespoons of lemon juice.

Simmer for about 30 minutes until the apricots are very soft.

Remove from the heat and stir in the sugar until fully dissolved.

Return to the heat and bring to a rapid boil for about 10 minutes and test for setting point.

Remove any scum. Pot and seal.

Label when cool.

Carrot Jam

Makes about 1.4 kg (3 lb)

A nice finishing touch is to stir in 1 tablespoon of brandy for each 450 g (1 lb) of jam before potting. This really lifts the flavour. Don't be tempted to add more though or you overwhelm the natural taste.

1.4 kg (3 lb) carrots
1.7 litres (3 pints) water
450 g (1 lb) sugar per 450 g (1 lb) of purée obtained
Rind and juice of 2 lemons per 450 g (1 lb) of purée
  obtained
140 ml (5 fl oz) pectin stock

Grate the carrots and put them in a saucepan with the water. Bring to the boil and simmer until soft.

Put through a blender or liquidizer, or press through a sieve.

Weigh the purée. For each 450 g (1 lb) of purée add 450g (1 lb) sugar and the rind and juice of 2 lemons.

Return the purée to the pan and warm through. Add the sugar, lemon rind and juice, stirring until the sugar has dissolved.

Bring to the boil and boil for about 30 minutes, stirring occasionally.

Stir in the pectin stock towards the end.

Pot into hot sterilized jars immediately and cover.

Label when cool.

Green Tomato Jam

Makes about 1.8 kg (4 lb)

If you're using actual lemons, grate the rind from them and squeeze out the juice. You can then add the grated rind in with the ginger to the muslin bag.

1.4 kg (3 lb) green tomatoes
900 g (2 lb) cooking apples
Juice of 2 lemons (or 4 tablespoons of bottled lemon juice)
28 g (1 oz) root ginger
1.4 kg (3 lb) sugar
A little water

Wash the tomatoes and cut into quarters. Peel and core the apples and cut into chunks.

Put the tomatoes and apples into a pan and add the lemon juice.

Bruise the ginger and tie in a muslin bag and place into the pan.

Cover with enough water to come to the level of the fruit.

Bring to the boil and then reduce to a simmer and cook until the fruit is tender.

Remove from the heat, add the sugar and stir until dissolved.

Return to the hob, bring back to the boil, then simmer, stirring occasionally, until thick.

Remove the muslin bag and pour into sterilized warm jars and cover.

4

MAKING MARMALADE

Marmalade making is very similar to jam making but the rind needs much longer cooking so more water is required. The fruit is simmered until the rind is soft and the volume of liquid has reduced by about half. Jelly marmalades are made in the same way but are strained through a jelly bag (see page 76) after the fruit has been cooked and strips of rind are then added.

Although the bitter Seville oranges with their short season of December to February in the shops are most popular, any citrus fruit can be used for making marmalade – bitter or sweet oranges, lemons, grapefruit, tangerines, satsumas, etc, on their own or in various combinations. You can use the marmalade process with other fruits such as quince where it serves to soften tough rinds.

We find that a great time to buy citrus fruits is just after Christmas. The supermarkets are loaded with oranges and Satsuma mandarin oranges that haven't sold before Christmas and are now going for a song.

Flavourings such as ginger, Armagnac, whisky, rum, brandy, treacle and apricots can be added but the citrus flavour must predominate. You'll be amazed how the addition of a little spirit can transform the flavour. It doesn't overwhelm so much as enhance the taste.

Since you are using the peel with marmalade, which is where pesticide residues tend to linger, it makes a lot of sense to buy organic fruits if you can afford to. In any case, wash the fruit thoroughly with a little washing up liquid in warm water – a soft nail brush helps. This removes any wax coatings as well as any dirt adhering to the peel. Rinse well though, we don't want washing up liquid flavoured marmalade.

The same equipment is required for making marmalade that is used for jams and jellies with the addition of a good sharp knife and a juice extractor, by which we mean the glass type one which you turn and squeeze the fruit – not the expensive machines!

You will also find that some weighing scales that are large enough to take your preserving pan and adjustable to compensate for the weight of the pan are really useful.

Pectin

The pectin in citrus fruit is contained in the white pith and pips. Extra acid is often added to ensure a good set as only about 450 g (1 lb) of fruit is used to make 1.4 kg (3 lb) of marmalade.

Preparation of Fruit

Wash and lightly scrub the fruit and dry thoroughly.

Slice or shred the fruit according to preference and recipe and, for thick marmalade, tie the pips in a muslin bag. If you dislike pith in your marmalade, remove it from the peel, chop roughly and add this in with the pips to the muslin bag.

For jelly marmalade it's always preferable to remove as much pith as possible from the peel. It can go back in with the fruit as it will be strained off later in the process.

Put the fruit, juice and other ingredients into a pan with the muslin bag and add water as per the recipe.

Thick Marmalade

Put all the ingredients into a pan with the pips in a muslin bag, bring to the boil and simmer gently until the peel is soft. This will take between 1½–2 hours. You can also use less water and boil in a pressure cooker on medium for about half the time but we find it more controllable to cook with an open pan on the hob.

Lift out the bag of pips, squeezing it against the side of the pan with a wooden spoon.

Test for pectin as described on page 30. If a large clot forms, the pectin is adequate to obtain a good set. If the clot is poor or thready, add the juice of two lemons to each 900 g (2 lb) fruit used and continue simmering the fruit until a good pectin clot is obtained.

Remove from the heat, and stir in the sugar until it has dissolved.

Return to the hob, bring to the boil and boil rapidly for 15–35 minutes until the marmalade sets when tested.

Test for setting just like jam – put a little marmalade onto a cold plate, cool and, if the marmalade wrinkles when touched with the finger, it is cooked sufficiently and will set. Always draw the pan away from the heat when testing for 'set', otherwise the marmalade may over cook.

Skim off any excess sugar scum using a perforated spoon, then add a knob of butter and stir in to reduce any remaining scum. Do this as soon as possible after the setting point has been reached as, if left much longer, the scum tends to cling to the pieces of peel.

Leave the marmalade to cool slightly so that the peel will not rise to the top of the jar.

Pour the marmalade into clean, dry, hot sterilized jars.

Put a circle of waxed paper, waxed side down, on the top of the marmalade.

Wipe the jars clean.

Cover with lids or cellophane covers whilst the marmalade is still hot.

Leave to cool and when quite cold label up, giving the type of marmalade and date when it was made.

Store in a cool, dark, dry place.

Jelly Marmalades

Wash the fruit carefully and remove the peel very thinly, removing as much pith as possible. Cut the peel into fine strips and tie in a piece of muslin. Cut the remaining fruit and pith into pieces and place in a bowl, together with the muslin bag.

Pour on the water and leave to soak overnight.

Transfer to a preserving pan, bring to the boil and simmer gently until the peel is soft and the contents of the pan have been reduced. This will take 1½–2 hours. Remove the bag of shredded peel after it has cooked for about an hour (it depends on the fruit) so that it does not over cook. Rinse it in cold water and set aside.

Turn the contents of the preserving pan into a jelly bag and leave to strain overnight.

Test for pectin (see page 30).

Measure the juice and heat it in a pan. Add 450g (1 lb)

warmed sugar to each 570 ml (1 pint) of juice, stir until all the sugar has dissolved. Add the shredded peel.

Bring to the boil and boil rapidly until the marmalade sets when tested.

Remove the scum and let the marmalade cool a little so that the peel does not rise to the top of the jelly.

Pour into clean, dry, hot sterilized jars.

Wipe the jars clean and cover with lids or cellophane covers whilst still hot.

Leave to cool and, when cold, label giving the type of marmalade and date on which it was made.

Store in a cool, dry place.

Seville Orange Marmalade

Makes about 4.5 kg (10 lb)

1.4 kg (3 lb) Seville oranges
Juice of 2 lemons
2.8 litres (5 pints) water
2.7 kg (6 lb) sugar

Wash and dry the fruit. Cut in half and squeeze out the juice. Remove the pips and tie these in a piece of muslin.

Slice or shred the oranges or coarsely chop in a food processor.

Put into a pan along with the lemon juice and water and the bag of pips. Bring to the boil and simmer gently until the peel is really soft. This will take between 1½–2 hours.

Lift out the bag of pips, squeezing it against the side of the pan with a wooden spoon.

Test for pectin (see page 30). If a large clot forms, the pectin is adequate to obtain a good set. If the clot is poor or thready, add the juice of another lemon and continue simmering the fruit until a good pectin clot is obtained.

Remove from the heat and stir in the sugar until it has dissolved.

Return to the hob, bring to the boil and boil rapidly for 15–35 minutes until the marmalade sets when tested.

Pot and seal whilst still hot.

Old English Marmalade

Makes about 2.7 kg (6 lb)

This is the traditional marmalade that takes advantage of the short season after Christmas when the bitter Seville oranges are in the shops.

900 kg (2 lb) Seville oranges
2 lemons
2.3 litres (4 pints) water
1.8 kg (4 lb) sugar – of which at least 450 g (1 lb)
  should be brown sugar

Wash and dry the fruit. Cut in half and squeeze out the juice. Remove the pips, inside skin and pith. Tie these in a piece of muslin.

Cut the peel and fruit chunkily.

Put into a pan with the muslin bag and the water. Bring to the boil and simmer gently until the peel is really soft and the volume has reduced to about half of its original bulk. This will take between 1½–2 hours.

Lift out the muslin bag, squeezing it against the side of the pan with a wooden spoon.

Test for pectin (see page 30). Remove from the heat and stir in the sugar until it has dissolved.

Return to the hob, bring to the boil and boil rapidly for 15–35 minutes until the marmalade sets when tested.

Allow to cool slightly, stir, and then pot and seal whilst still hot.

Tangerine Jelly Marmalade
Estimating the yield from any jelly is difficult as it depends on the amount of juice extracted

This is a useful recipe for taking advantage of the bargain offers on tangerines in the shops after Christmas.

900 g (2 lb) tangerines
1 or 2 lemons and 1 grapefruit with combined weight of 350 g (12 oz)
2.6 litres (4½ pints) water
450 g (1 lb) sugar per 570ml (1 pint) of juice obtained

Wash and dry the fruit. Remove the peel from the tangerines thinly and remove the pith. Shred finely. Tie the shreds in a muslin bag.

Peel the lemons and grapefruit and finely dice. Chop up all the fruit and put into a bowl with the diced peel, pith and muslin bag. Pour on the water and leave to soak overnight.

Transfer to a preserving pan, bring to the boil and simmer gently for about 2 hours, removing the tangerine shreds after about 40 minutes and put in a sieve. Rinse the tangerine shreds under cold running water and then transfer to a bowl of cold water.

Turn the contents of the preserving pan into a jelly bag and leave to strain for several hours or overnight.

Test for pectin (see page 30).

Measure the juice and heat it in a pan. Add 450 g (1 lb) of warmed sugar to each 570 ml (1 pint) of juice, stir until all the sugar has dissolved. Add the shredded peel.

Bring to the boil and boil rapidly until the marmalade sets when tested.

Remove the scum and let the marmalade cool a little so that the peel does not rise to the top of the jelly.

Pour into clean, dry, hot sterilized jars.

Wipe the jars clean and cover with lids or cellophane covers whilst still hot.

Leave to cool and, when cold, label giving the type of marmalade and date on which it was made.

Store in a cool, dry place.

Lemon or Lime Jelly Marmalade

Estimating the yield from any jelly is difficult as it depends on the amount of juice extracted

Just as with the Lemon or Lime Marmalade (page 72), you can use either fruit or a mixture of both. A little brandy will really lift the flavour. Varying a favourite recipe slightly each time helps keep the taste fresh and interesting.

1.4 kg (3 lb) lemons or limes
2.8 litres (5 pints) water
450 g (1 lb) sugar per 570ml (1 pint) of juice obtained

Wash the fruit carefully and remove the peel very thinly. Cut the peel into fine strips and tie in a piece of muslin.

Cut the remaining fruit and pith into pieces and place in a bowl, together with the muslin bag. Pour on the water and leave to soak overnight.

Transfer to a preserving pan and bring to the boil and simmer gently until the peel is soft and the contents of the pan have been reduced. This will take 1½–2 hours.

Remove the bag of shredded peel, rinse under cold water and put aside.

Turn the contents of the preserving pan into a jelly bag and leave to strain for several hours or overnight.

Test for pectin (see page 30).

Measure the juice and heat it in a pan. Add 450 g (1 lb) warmed sugar to each 570 ml (1 pint) of juice, stirring until all the sugar has dissolved. Add the shredded peel.

Bring to the boil and boil rapidly until the marmalade sets when tested.

Remove the scum and let the marmalade cool a little so that the peel does not rise to the top of the jelly.

Pour into clean, dry, hot sterilized jars.

Wipe the jars clean and cover with lids or cellophane covers whilst still hot.

Leave to cover and, when cold, label giving the type of marmalade and date on which it was made.

Store in a cool, dry place.

Orange Jelly Marmalade

*Estimating the yield from any jelly is difficult as it depends
on the amount of juice extracted*

**900 g (2 lb) Seville or sweet oranges or a mixture of
  both**
2 lemons
2.3 litres (4 pints) water
450 g (1 lb) sugar per 570ml (1 pint) of juice obtained

Wash the fruit carefully and remove the peel very
thinly. Cut the peel into fine strips and tie in a piece of
muslin.

Cut the remaining fruit and pith into pieces and place in a
bowl, together with the muslin bag. Pour on the water and
leave to soak overnight.

Bring to the boil and simmer gently until the peel is soft
and the contents of the pan have been reduced. This will
take 1½–2 hours.

Remove the bag of shredded peel (you may wish to do this
a little earlier if it is already tender to prevent it over-
cooking), rinse under cold water and put aside.

Turn the contents of the preserving pan into a jelly bag and
leave to strain for several hours or overnight.

Test for pectin (see page 30).

Measure the juice and heat it in a pan. Add 450 g (1 lb)
warmed sugar to each 570 ml (1 pint) of juice, stirring until
all the sugar has dissolved. Add the shredded peel.

Bring to the boil and boil rapidly until the marmalade sets
when tested.

Remove the scum and let the marmalade cool a little so that the peel does not rise to the top of the jelly.

Pour into clean, dry, hot sterilized jars.

Wipe the jars clean and cover with lids or cellophane covers whilst still hot.

Leave to cover and, when cold, label giving the type of marmalade and date on which it was made.

Store in a cool, dry place.

Lemon or Lime Marmalade

Makes about 2.7 kg (6 lb)

You can make this marmalade with either limes or lemons or a mixture of both, which works well.

900 g (2 lb) lemons or limes
2.3 litres (4 pints) water
1.8 kg (4 lb) sugar

Wash and dry the fruit. Cut in half and squeeze out the juice. Remove the pips and tie these in a piece of muslin.

Slice or shred the fruit.

Put into a pan along with the juice, water and the bag of pips. Bring to the boil and simmer gently until the peel is really soft. This will take between 1½–2 hours.

Lift out the bag of pips, squeezing it against the side of the pan with a wooden spoon.

Test for pectin (see page 30). This is rarely lacking.

Remove from the heat and stir in the sugar until it has dissolved.

Return to the hob, bring to the boil and boil rapidly for 15–35 minutes until the marmalade sets when tested.

Remove any scum and leave to cool slightly.

Stir, pot and seal whilst still hot.

Pink Grapefruit with Armagnac Marmalade

Makes about 3.6 kg (8 lb)

Other alcohol flavourings than Armagnac go well in marmalades, particularly dark rum, brandy and whisky, but don't use more than 1 or 2 tablespoons to each 450 g (1 lb) or it masks the citrus taste. We had problems in getting a good set once with this marmalade and ended up having to tip it out of the jars the next day, re-heating and stirring in two sachets (26 g) of Silver Spoon pectin which solved it.

1.4 kg (3 lb) pink grapefruit
Juice of 2 lemons
3.4 litres (6 pints) water
2.7 kg (6 lb) sugar

Wash and dry the fruit. Cut in half and slice or shred – preferably on a plate to catch the juice. Remove the pips and tie these in a piece of muslin.

Put into a pan along with the juice, water and the bag of pips. Bring to the boil and simmer gently until the peel is really soft. This will take between 1½–2 hours.

Lift out the bag of pips, squeezing it against the side of the pan with a wooden spoon.

Test for pectin (see page 30). Remove from the heat and stir in the sugar until it has dissolved.

Return to the hob, bring to the boil and boil rapidly for 15–35 minutes until the marmalade sets when tested. Remove any scum and leave to cool slightly.

Add 1 tablespoon of Armagnac for each 450 g (1 lb) and stir. Pot and seal whilst still warm.

5

JELLIES

The process of making jellies is very similar to that of jams except there is the additional stage after the initial boiling of the fruit – straining the fruit pulp through a jelly bag. Jelly bags are usually made of nylon or cotton and fairly easy to obtain. On the internet we found a useful drip stand frame that holds the bag above a bowl. You can't really suspend the bag overnight holding it in your hands so before we found this we used to improvise.

The first time we upturned a kitchen stool and tied treble folded muslin to the legs above the side pieces. It worked remarkably well until we moved house and the stools stayed behind with the breakfast bar. See Fig. 3 overleaf.

Using a piece of plywood as a base and some upright dowels, we managed to fashion a drip stand using coat hanger wire tied to screws in the dowels to make side supports. The folded muslin jelly bag was then tied to that. A bit Heath Robinson, but it worked well. The problem was it took up a lot of room in the cupboard. The commercial drip stand folds flat for storage.

Whatever support method you use, do wash the bag out thoroughly after use and scald with boiling water before use to sterilize.

Don't squeeze the bag to hasten the process as this tends to make the final jelly cloudy. The 'perfect' jelly should be bright and clear.

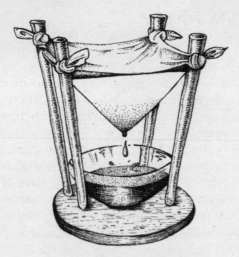

Fig. 3. An improvised jelly bag.

It's misleading to try and estimate the yield for jellies as it depends on how much juice you manage to extract. As a rough rule of the thumb, you'll get 2.3 kg (5 lb) of jelly for each 1.4 kg (3 lb) of sugar used.

Redcurrant Jelly

*Estimating the yield from any jelly is difficult as it depends
on the amount of juice extracted*

This is the basic currant recipe and instead of redcurrants
you can use blackcurrants or even white currants, although
they have an inferior flavour. Currants are rich in pectin so
setting should not be a problem.

Redcurrant jelly is a traditional accompaniment to lamb
but in Scandinavia, where they often tend to have sweet
accompaniments with their meat, they have lingonberry
jelly with venison and even meatballs. You cannot, as far as
we know, buy lingonberries in Britain but you can buy the
plants and grow them. Delicious.

1.8 kg (4 lb) redcurrants
1.7 litres (3 pints) water
450 g (1 lb) sugar per 570 ml (1 pint) of juice obtained

Wash and drain the redcurrants. Pick over to remove any
unsound fruit but do not remove the stalks.

Put the fruit into a pan with the water and simmer until the
fruit is pulpy.

Test for pectin (see page 30). Turn into a jelly bag and
leave to strain for 3–4 hours.

Measure the juice and heat in a pan. Add 450 g (1 lb)
warmed sugar to each 570 ml (1 pint) of juice, stirring until
the sugar has dissolved.

Bring to the boil and boil rapidly until the jelly sets when
tested. Remove the scum and pot into hot sterilized jars
and seal. Label when cool.

Blackberry Jelly

Estimating the yield from any jelly is difficult as it depends on the amount of juice extracted

As with blackberry jam, you can substitute crab apples for the cooking apples in this recipe. It's also the basis for elderberry jelly. With that, we achieved the best result by replacing half the blackberries with elderberries rather than all of them.

Hawthorn or rowan (mountain ash) berries can also be used but not combined with the blackberries. The apples tend to reduce the bitterness of the berries.

450 g (1 lb) cooking apples
1.8 kg (4 lb) blackberries
690 ml (1¼ pints) water
Juice of 1 lemon
340 g (¾ lb) sugar per 570 ml (1 pint) of juice obtained

Wash and wipe the apples, cut into quarters, but do not remove the skins or cores.

Wash and drain the blackberries and pick over to remove any unsound fruit and stalks.

Put the apples into a pan with the water and lemon juice and simmer until pulpy.

Add the blackberries and continue simmering until the blackberries are soft.

Test for pectin (see page 30).

Turn into a jelly bag and leave overnight to strain.

Measure the juice and heat in a pan.

Add 340 g (¾ lb) warmed sugar to each 570 ml (1 pint) of juice, stirring until all the sugar has dissolved.

Bring to the boil and boil rapidly until the jelly sets when tested.

Remove the scum.

Pot into hot sterilized jars and seal. Label when cool.

Cranberry Jelly

*Estimating the yield from any jelly is difficult as it depends
on the amount of juice extracted*

Cranberries are, of course, the traditional Christmas
accompaniment to the turkey. To make it really special,
put some jelly into an oven proof dish and warm slightly
(we use the microwave on low for a few seconds) then mix
in a little brandy.

900 g (2 lb) cranberries
430 ml (¾ pint) water
450 g (1 lb) sugar per 570 ml (1 pint) of juice obtained

Wash and drain the cranberries.

Put the cranberries into a pan with the water and bring to
the boil. Simmer until the skins have broken.

Test for pectin (see page 30).

Turn into a jelly bag and leave to strain for 3–4 hours.

Measure the juice and heat in a pan.

Add 450 g (1 lb) warmed sugar to each 570 ml (1 pint) of
juice, stirring until the sugar has dissolved.

Bring to the boil and boil rapidly until the jelly sets when
tested.

Remove the scum.

Pot into hot sterilized jars and seal. Label when cool.

Raspberry Jelly

Estimating the yield from any jelly is difficult as it depends on the amount of juice extracted

The beauty of this is that you can enjoy all the flavour of raspberry jam without the annoying little pips getting stuck in your teeth.

1.8 kg (4 lb) raspberries
570 ml (1 pint) water
340 g (¾ lb) sugar per 570 ml (1 pint) of juice obtained

Wash and drain the raspberries.

Pick over to remove any unsound fruit and stalks.

Put into a pan with the water and simmer until the fruit is soft and pulpy.

Test for pectin (see page 30).

Turn into a jelly bag and leave to strain overnight.

Measure the juice and heat in a pan.

Add 340 g (¾ lb) warmed sugar per 570 ml (1 pint) of juice, stirring until all the sugar has dissolved.

Bring to the boil and boil rapidly until the jelly sets when tested.

Remove the scum.

Pot into hot sterilized jars and seal. Label when cool.

Gooseberry Jelly

Estimating the yield from any jelly is difficult as it depends on the amount of juice extracted

1.8 kg (4 lb) gooseberries
1.1 litres (2 pints) water
450 g (1 lb) sugar per 570 ml (1 pint) of juice obtained

Wash and drain the gooseberries.

Pick over to remove any unsound fruit but do not top and tail.

Put into a pan with the water and simmer until the fruit is soft and pulpy.

Test for pectin (see page 30).

Turn into a jelly bag and leave overnight to strain.

Measure the juice and heat in a pan.

Add 450 g (1 lb) warmed sugar to each 570 ml (1 pint) of juice, stirring until all the sugar has dissolved.

Bring to the boil and boil rapidly until the jelly sets when tested.

Remove the scum.

Pot into hot sterilized jars and seal. Label when cool.

Mint Jelly

Estimating the yield from any jelly is difficult as it depends on the amount of juice extracted

This makes a different accompaniment for lamb from the traditional mint sauce. It's really nice on new potatoes as well. It works best with caster sugar but you can always put some granulated sugar through a food processor or grinder to make your own.

1.8 kg (4 lb) cooking apples
1.1 litres (2 pints) water
1 bundle fresh mint
450 g (1 lb) caster sugar per 570 ml (1 pint) of juice
Few drops of green food colouring (optional)

Wash the apples and cut into pieces. Do not remove the cores or peel. Put into a pan with the water and a few sprigs of mint. Simmer slowly until soft and pulpy.

Test for pectin (see page 30).

Turn into a jelly bag and leave overnight to strain.

Measure the juice, put it into a pan and add 450 g (1 lb) warmed caster sugar to each 570 ml (1 pint) of juice. Heat gently until all the sugar has dissolved.

Bring to the boil, chop up the rest of the mint finely and add about two teaspoons of mint to each 570 ml (1 pint) of juice.

Boil rapidly until the jelly sets when tested.

Add a few drops of green food colouring if liked. Pot into hot sterilized jars and seal. Label when cool.

Apple and Rosemary Jelly

Estimating the yield from any jelly is difficult as it depends on the amount of juice extracted

A few drops of green food colouring can be added during the cooking process if you like. This makes a nice alternative to the mint jelly for lamb.

1.4 kg (3 lb) crab or cooking apples
570 ml (1 pint) water
2 tablespoons rosemary leaves
4 tablespoons cider vinegar
450 g (1 lb) sugar per 570 ml (1 pint) of juice obtained

Wash the apples and wipe. Cut into quarters but do not remove the skins or cores.

Put the fruit into a pan with the water, rosemary leaves and cider vinegar.

Simmer until the fruit is pulpy.

Test for pectin (see page 30).

Turn into a jelly bag and leave to strain overnight.

Measure the juice and heat in a pan.

Add 450 g (1 lb) warmed sugar to each 570 ml (1 pint) juice, stirring until all the sugar has dissolved.

Bring to the boil and boil rapidly until the jelly sets when tested.

Remove the scum. Pot into hot sterilized jars and seal. Label when cool.

Apple Jelly

*Estimating the yield from any jelly is difficult as it depends
on the amount of juice extracted*

Apple Jelly is a bit bland on its own so additional flavouring
is added by picking from the suggestions below or to suit
your own taste. Apple carries flavour really well.

1.8 kg (4 lb) crab or cooking apples
1.1 litres (2 pints) water
**Stick cinnamon/a few cloves/root ginger/strips of
  lemon rind/fresh mint**
**450 g (1 lb) sugar per 570 ml (1 pint) of juice
  obtained**

Wash the apples and wipe. Cut into quarters but do not
remove the skins or cores.

Put the fruit into a pan with the water and the choice of
additional flavouring (stick of cinnamon or a few cloves or
root ginger or strips of lemon rind or fresh mint) tied in a
piece of muslin. Simmer until the fruit is pulpy.

Test for pectin (see page 30).

Remove the flavouring ingredients. Turn into a jelly bag
and leave to strain overnight.

Measure the juice and heat in a pan. Add 450 g (1 lb)
warmed sugar to each 570 ml (1 pint) juice, stirring until
all the sugar has dissolved.

Bring to the boil and boil rapidly until the jelly sets when
tested.

Remove the scum. Pot into hot sterilized jars and seal.
Label when cool.

6

CONSERVES

Conserves take ordinary jams to a whole new level. We move beyond preserving into creating delicious confections that are definitely not going to help you lose weight!

They follow the same principles as jam but the fruit stays whole, or at the size into which it is cut, and the fruit is suspended in a syrup which does not set as stiffly as in a jam.

As conserves are considered much more of a luxury than an ordinary jam, it gives the opportunity to incorporate additional flavour and texture in the form of nuts, alcohol and more unusual fruits. The storage life tends to be shorter and they are best used within six months.

Generally pot into smaller jars, as you will be tempted to finish the jar when it's opened.

These are our absolute favourites and make fantastic presents as well, if you can part with them.

Strawberry Conserve

Makes about 1.4 kg (3 lb)

This does take strawberry jam to a new level and is well worth the extra time and trouble in the making.

900 g (2 lb) either very small strawberries or halved hulled medium strawberries, slightly under-ripe
900 g (2 lb) sugar
Juice of 1 lemon (or 2 tablespoons of bottled lemon juice)

Place alternate layers of strawberries and sugar into a bowl; add the lemon juice, cover and leave to stand overnight.

Next day, transfer the fruit and sugar to a pan, bring slowly to the boil and simmer for 5 minutes. Pour back into the bowl, cover and leave again for another day.

Finally, transfer to a pan, bring to the boil and simmer until setting point is reached.

Remove from the heat and leave to cool a little until the fruit begins to sink in the syrup.

Stir and pour into small, hot sterilized jars and cover immediately. Label when cool.

Peach Conserve with Brandy

Makes about 2.3 kg (5 lb)

**1.4 kg (3 lb) ripe peaches (weight after stones have
  been removed)
112 g (4 oz) chopped walnuts or almonds
Finely grated rind and juice of 1 lemon
Pinch of ground cinnamon
1.125 kg (2½ lb) sugar
5 tablespoons brandy
285 ml (½ pint) pectin stock (see page 29)**

Peel, stone and cut the peaches into smallish pieces, collecting all of the juice.

Put into a pan with the nuts, lemon rind and juice and a pinch of ground cinnamon.

Gently heat and add the sugar, stirring until it has dissolved and the fruit is well coated.

Bring to the boil and boil for about 2 minutes.

Remove from the heat and stir in the brandy and pectin stock.

Leave to cool slightly for 5 minutes and then stir again.

Pour into hot, sterilized jars and cover.

Label when cool.

Grape and Port Conserve

Makes about 1.125 kg (2½ lb)

For a variation, stir in some glacé cherries. If you use red sweet grapes add a couple of tablespoons of lemon juice.

900 g (2 lb) small seedless red or green grapes
570 ml (1 pint) port
900 g (2 lb) sugar

Wash the grapes and remove any stalks.

Put into a pan with the port.

Heat gently and then add the sugar, stirring until the sugar has dissolved.

Bring to the boil, stirring often until the grapes are soft but still intact and the syrup thick.

Allow to cool slightly, stir to redistribute the fruit, then pour into small, hot sterilized jars and seal.

Label when cool.

Black Cherry Conserve

Makes about 750 g (1½–2 lb)

We always stir in about 4 tablespoons of brandy to this conserve but it's not really necessary as the black cherries have so much flavour. The 'set' on this conserve is always pretty loose.

560 g (1¼ lb) black cherries, weight when stoned
450 g (1 lb) sugar
2 tablespoons lemon juice

Put the cherries into a bowl along with any juice that came out whilst stoning, stir in the sugar and cover and leave for several hours or overnight.

Transfer to a pan and simmer over a low heat, stirring, until the sugar has dissolved. Add the lemon juice and bring to the boil steadily and boil until setting point is reached.

Allow to cool slightly and stir to re-distribute the cherries.

Pour into hot, sterilized jars and cover.

Label when cool.

Tayberry Conserve

Makes about 1.4 kg (3 lb)

We rarely add anything in the form of alcohol to this conserve but have been told that a couple of tablespoons of vodka works wonders!

Making the syrup before cooking and pouring over the fruit works well for most berry fruit as it helps prevent them from breaking up and going mushy. The same recipe can be used for raspberries and ripe strawberries. With the strawberries, you'll probably need to hull and cut in half. Instead of lemon juice, you can use double the amount of redcurrant juice. Blackberries don't work very well because of their hard pips.

900 g (2 lb) tayberries
4 tablespoons lemon juice
900 g (2 lb) sugar

Place the tayberries into a heat-proof bowl or basin.

Put the lemon juice and sugar into a pan and stir over a very low heat until the sugar has dissolved and then bring to the boil.

Pour the hot syrup over the tayberries, stir so they are all coated, cover and put aside for a few hours.

Transfer the berries and syrup back to a pan and bring slowly back to the boil.

Boil for about 4–5 minutes or until setting point is reached.

Allow to cool slightly and stir.

Pour into hot, sterilized jars and cover. Label when cool.

7

FRUIT CURDS

A fruit curd is not strictly speaking a preserve, although you'll find lemon curd on the shop shelf next to the jams. No matter, curds are delicious and versatile. They make a great filling for tarts and cakes as well as thickly spread on bread and butter.

Because of the lightly cooked eggs in them, there are health implications and homemade curds are probably best avoided by pregnant women, babies, younger children and the elderly or anyone who is at particular risk from salmonella. It is a very small risk, but nonetheless a risk.

Although you can use any eggs in curds, the best results will be obtained by using really fresh, organic free-range eggs. Not only is the flavour improved but the colour is better as well. If you keep hens, then here's the perfect way to use up a few spare eggs.

Be careful when breaking the eggs, as you don't want any egg shell – especially shell with dirt on – in the curd. Washing the eggs before you start is probably a good idea, as well.

Your fruit curd will also benefit from using good quality butter, which must be unsalted.

Be aware that homemade curds don't store for long. They're best kept in the refrigerator and eaten within two or three weeks at most. Luckily that isn't usually a problem.

Unlike jams which set, curds just become thicker as they cool. Don't worry if it seems a little runny when you pot up but, if at the end of the cooking time, the curd seems very thin, add another egg yolk and cook for a further 5–10 minutes.

Pay special attention to sterilizing the jars for fruit curds. Unlike shop made, you're not using preservatives and are eating an absolutely natural product that contains lightly cooked egg. Do remember that the curd will thicken as it cools and will also shrink, thus filling right to the top of the jar is important and a waxed paper disc on the top is another line of defence against moulds.

The recipes call for caster sugar as this is finer and dissolves more easily. You can save some money by making your own. Just put ordinary granulated sugar into the food processor and give it a whiz.

Lemon Curd

Makes about 900 g (2 lb)

This is usually the only fruit curd you find in the shops. You'll probably realize that this is more expensive to make than to buy from the shops ready made. However, once you taste it, you'll never buy it from the shop again!

4 large lemons
6 free-range eggs, well beaten
450 g (1 lb) caster sugar
112 g (4 oz) unsalted butter

Wash the lemons and remove very thin strips of rind from two of them.

Cut in half and squeeze out the juice, removing any pips.

Put the juice and rind, beaten eggs and other ingredients into a double saucepan (or heatproof-bowl over a pan of hot water) on low heat and heat gently until all the sugar has dissolved, stirring all the time.

Continue heating, stirring all the time, for about 20 minutes or until the mixture thickens.

Remove the rind.

Turn into hot clean jars and seal at once.

Lime Curd

Makes about 675 g (1½ lb)

Juice and rind from 6 limes
Juice from 1 lemon
4 free-range eggs, well beaten
340 g (12 oz) caster sugar
112 g (4 oz) unsalted butter

Wash the limes and lemon. Finely grate the rind from the limes.

Cut in half and squeeze out the juice, removing any pips.

Put the juice and rind, beaten eggs and other ingredients into a double saucepan or heatproof-bowl over a pan of hot water) on low heat and heat gently until all the sugar has dissolved.

Continue heating, stirring often, for about 20 minutes or until the mixture thickens.

Remove the rind.

Turn into hot, clean, sterilized jars and seal at once.

Label when cool.

Apricot Curd

Easily makes 900 g (2 lb)

675 g (1½ lb) fresh apricots or 1 lb (450 g) dried
112 g (4 oz) unsalted butter
4 free-range eggs
450 g (1 lb) caster sugar
Juice of 2 lemons

Wash fresh apricots in hot water. Soak dried apricots for 24 hours in water.

Simmer the apricots in a pan with just enough water to prevent them burning. When soft, push through a strainer into a medium-sized mixing bowl, pressing down on the fruit with a wooden spoon. Throw away the skins left in the strainer.

Put another heatproof bowl over a pan of simmering water and melt the butter. Beat the eggs lightly and stir into the bowl with the sugar, apricot purée and the juice of the lemons.

Heat the mixture, stirring frequently, for 25–30 minutes or until it thickens.

Remove the bowl from the heat and pour the curd into clean, dry, warm, sterilized jars.

Seal and cover.

Label with date and contents when fully cooled.

Blackberry Curd

Makes about 2.3 kg (5 lb)

1.8 kg (4 lb) blackberries
675 g (1½ lb) cooking or crab apples
285 ml (½ pint) water
225 g (8 oz) unsalted butter
6 free-range eggs
Juice of 3 lemons
1.8 kg (4 lb) sugar

Pick over the blackberries, peel, core and dice the apples and place in a large saucepan with 285 ml (½ pint) water. Bring to the boil over a high heat. Reduce the heat, cover and simmer for about 20 minutes until the fruit is soft.

Remove from the heat and push the fruit through a strainer into a medium-sized mixing bowl, pressing down on the fruit with a wooden spoon.

Put another heatproof bowl over a pan of simmering water and melt the butter. Beat the eggs lightly and stir into the bowl with the lemon juice, sugar and blackberry and apple purée.

Heat the mixture, stirring frequently, for 25–30 minutes or until it thickens.

Remove the bowl from the heat and pour the curd into clean, dry, warm, sterilized jars.

Seal and cover.

Label with date and contents when fully cooled.

Gooseberry Curd

Makes about 900 g (2 lb)

900 g (2 lb) gooseberries
50 ml (2 fl oz) water
2 oz (56 g) unsalted butter
3 free-range eggs
450 g (1 lb) sugar

Top and tail the gooseberries and place in a large saucepan with 50 ml (2 fl oz) water. Bring to the boil over a high heat. Reduce the heat, cover and simmer for about 20 minutes until the gooseberries are soft and mushy.

Remove from the heat and push the gooseberries through a strainer into a medium-sized mixing bowl, pressing down on the fruit with a wooden spoon. Throw away the skins left in the strainer.

Put another heatproof bowl over a pan of simmering water and melt the butter. Beat the eggs lightly and stir into the bowl with the sugar and gooseberry purée.

Heat the mixture, stirring frequently, for 25–30 minutes or until it thickens.

Remove the bowl from the heat and pour the curd into clean, dry, warm, sterilized jars.

Seal and cover.

Label with date and contents when fully cooled.

Orange Curd

Makes about 900 g (2 lb)

3 oranges
1 lemon
6 free-range eggs, well beaten
1 lb (450 g) caster sugar
112 g (4 oz) unsalted butter

Wash the oranges and lemon and remove very thin strips of rind from one orange and the lemon.

Cut the fruit in half and squeeze out the juice, removing any pips.

Put the juice and rind, beaten eggs and other ingredients into a double saucepan (or heatproof-bowl over a pan of hot water) on low heat and heat gently until all the sugar has dissolved.

Continue heating, stirring frequently, for about 20 minutes or until the mixture thickens.

Remove the rind.

Turn into hot, clean jars and seal at once.

8

FRUIT BUTTERS

Fruit butters and fruit cheeses are old-fashioned names for preserves made with fruit purée and sugar. Generally the fruits used for jellies are also the best ones for butter and cheeses and they can even be made from the pulp left in the jelly bag after the juice has dripped. Two products from one fruit!

The same equipment is required as for jam making, with the addition of a fine nylon or plastic sieve.

Fruit butters are soft and spreadable. They are a particularly useful way for dealing with a glut of wild fruits and, as less sugar is required for this sort of preserve, they are very economical.

They make a great filling for sponge cakes and tarts as well as being used as a spread like jam.

Note that fruit butters don't keep very well, especially when the lower amount of sugar is used, and need to be refrigerated.

You know that fruit butters are ready when there is no liquid visible and the surface is creamy.

Spiced Apple Butter

Makes about 2.7 kg (6 lb)

2.7 kg (6 lb) crab apples (or windfalls)
1.1 litres (2 pints) water
1.1 litres (2 pints) dry cider
340 g (¾ lb) sugar per 450 g (1 lb) of purée obtained
1 teaspoon ground cinnamon
1 teaspoon ground cloves
½ teaspoon ground allspice
Rind of ½ a lemon, grated finely

Wash the apples, remove any bruised bits and cut into pieces.

Place in a stainless steel or enamelled pan with the water and cider.

Bring to the boil, then simmer until the apples are very soft.

Push the fruit and cooking liquid through a fine sieve and weigh the purée.

Return the purée to the pan and simmer until it has reduced by about one-third or until thick.

Stir in 340 g (¾ lb) of sugar for each 450 g (l lb) of purée. Once the sugar has dissolved, add the cinnamon, cloves, allspice and lemon rind, bring to the boil, then reduce to a simmer, stirring occasionally, and cook until thick and creamy and no liquid remains but it's of a consistency that the butter can still be spread from cold.

Spoon into clean, dry, warm, sterilized jars. Cover and seal with an airtight lid. Label with date and contents when fully cooled.

Blackcurrant Butter

Makes about 1.8 kg (4 lb)

1.8 kg (4 lb) blackcurrants
1.7 litres (3 pints) water
225–340 g (½–¾ lb) sugar per 450 g (1 lb) of purée
   obtained

Wash the fruit and place in a large saucepan with the water.

Bring to the boil, then simmer, very gently or their skins will get tough, until the blackcurrants are very soft.

Push the fruit and cooking liquid through a fine sieve and weigh the purée.

Return the purée to the pan and simmer until it has reduced by about one-third or until thick.

Stir in 225–340 g (½–¾ lb) of sugar for each 450 g (l lb) of purée. Once the sugar has dissolved, bring to the boil, then reduce to a simmer, stirring occasionally, until thick and creamy with no visible liquid remaining but of a consistency that the butter can still be spread from cold.

Spoon into clean, dry, warm, sterilized jars.

Cover and seal with an airtight lid.

Label with date and contents when fully cooled.

Gooseberry Butter

Makes about 1.8 kg (4 lb)

1.8 kg (4 lb) ripe gooseberries
430 ml (¾ pint) water
340 g (¾ lb) sugar per 450 g (1 lb) of purée obtained

Top, tail and wash the fruit and place in a large saucepan with the water.

Bring to the boil and then simmer until the gooseberries are soft.

Push the fruit and cooking liquid through a fine sieve and weigh the purée.

Return the purée to the pan and simmer until it has reduced by about one-third or until thick.

Stir in 340 g (¾ lb) of sugar for each 450 g (l lb) of purée. Once the sugar has dissolved, bring to the boil, then reduce to a simmer, stirring occasionally, and cook until thick and creamy with no visible liquid remaining but the butter can still be spread from cold.

Spoon into clean, dry, warm, sterilized jars.

Cover and seal with an airtight lid.

Label with date and contents when fully cooled.

Fig. 4. Pushing the pulp or purée through a sieve.

9

FRUIT CHEESES

The main difference between fruit butters and fruit cheeses is the consistency. Whereas butters are spreadable, cheeses are firmer, like cheese. This is mainly due to them having more sugar content. The higher level of sugar also means that they keep longer than fruit butters.

They can be used as a sweet accompaniment, rather like a sweet pickle with cheese, or you can even make sweets from them. Once made, you can pour into small wide mouthed jars and treat as jam or you can use biscuit moulds to create shapes like stars and circles. You can roll into tubes or even small balls in your hands to make small treats.

If you wish to dry them further, put them into a very low oven on a baking tray and then sprinkle with caster sugar. Wrap individually and pack in an airtight tin for a very unusual present.

You can even take it one step further and dip your dried fruit cheese sweets in chocolate. The contrast between a dark, bitter high-cocoa chocolate and the sweet fruit cheese centre is sublime.

Fruit cheeses are ready when you can draw a spoon across the top and leave a clean line.

Damson Cheese

Makes about 2.7 kg (6 lb)

2.7 kg (6 lb) damsons
285 ml (½ pint) water
450 g (1 lb) sugar per 450 g (1 lb) of purée obtained
2 teaspoons ground allspice

Wash the damsons and put them into a large saucepan with the water.

Bring to the boil, reduce the heat, cover and simmer until the damsons are tender.

Pour the mixture through a sieve over a large bowl and press through using the back of a wooden spoon.

Measure the fruit purée and allow 450 g (1 lb) of sugar to each 450 g (1 lb) of purée.

Return the purée to the pan, add the sugar and ground allspice. Stir frequently until the sugar has dissolved.

Bring to the boil, reduce the heat and continue cooking and stirring until very thick.

Pour into small, clean, dry, warm sterilized jars or moulds, cover and seal or make into sweets as described on page 107.

Label with contents and date when fully cool.

Blackberry Cheese

Makes about 1.8 kg (4 lb)

900 g (2 lb) cooking or crab apples
1.8 kg (4 lb) blackberries
570 ml (1 pint) water
450 g (1 lb) sugar per 450 g (1 lb) of purée obtained

Wash, peel and chop the apples, wash and drain the black-berries, and put them into a large saucepan with the water.

Bring to the boil, reduce the heat, cover and simmer until the fruit is very soft.

Squash it occasionally with the back of a wooden spoon to mix the fruit and release the juice.

Pour the mixture through a sieve over a large bowl and press through using the back of a wooden spoon.

Measure the fruit purée and allow 450 g (1 lb) of sugar to each 450 g (1 lb) of purée.

Return the purée to a clean pan, pour in the sugar and heat gently until it has dissolved.

Bring to the boil, reduce the heat and simmer until the cheese is thick.

Pour into small, clean, dry, warm sterilized jars or moulds, cover and seal or make into sweets as described on page 107.

Label with contents and date when fully cool.

Cranberry Cheese

Makes about 2.7 kg (6 lb)

2.7 kg (6 lb) cranberries
1 litre (1¾ pints) water
450 g (1 lb) sugar per 450 g (1 lb) of purée obtained
Juice and finely grated rind of 1 orange
1 tablespoon lemon juice
1 teaspoon cinnamon

Wash and trim the cranberries and put them into a large saucepan with the water.

Bring to the boil, reduce the heat, cover and simmer until the cranberries are very soft. Squash them occasionally with the back of a wooden spoon to release the juice.

Pour the mixture through a sieve over a large bowl and press through using the back of a wooden spoon.

Measure the fruit purée and allow 450 g (1 lb) of sugar to each 450 g (1 lb) of purée.

Return the purée to a clean pan. If it is very liquid, boil it for a few minutes and allow to reduce slightly.

Stir in the sugar and heat gently until it has dissolved. Add the finely grated orange rind and juice, lemon juice and cinnamon. Bring to the boil, reduce the heat and simmer until the cheese is fairly stiff.

Pour into small, clean, dry, warm sterilized jars or moulds, cover and seal or make into sweets as described on page 107.

Label with contents and date when fully cool.

10

CHUTNEYS

The scope of chutneys is endless and the combinations and permutations can be varied according to personal taste and the ingredients available. They can be sweet or sour, hot or mild and the range of ingredients is almost unlimited as well. They can be made from fruits or vegetables, or a mixture of the two.

Better still, because the ingredients are going to be chopped, cooked, mixed with spices, vinegar and other ingredients and often reduced to a smooth pulp, you don't have to be fussy about the quality of the fruits and vegetables. Misshapen or damaged fruits can be used.

They're good for using up end of season produce as well. Windfall apples, green tomatoes and the last of the rhubarb can all be converted into an appetizing chutney. To the chutney's base ingredients you add various spices and other fruits like raisins, sultanas, dates and vegetables such as onion and garlic for the flavour. The vinegars, sugar and salt are there not just for the flavour but they are also the preservative.

Although we tend to think of chutney as a condiment, mango chutney with a curry for example, it can provide a substantial portion of a meal. We enjoy chicken fillets cooked in green tomato chutney with plain rice as a meal. It's our own bottled 'cook in' sauce.

One point to bear in mind is that the flavour of a chutney improves with age. Most chutneys take at least a couple of months for the full flavour to develop and mature. Personally, we would never even try one of our chutneys until it has sat maturing for three months.

We're often asked how long chutneys should keep for. The answer is not that simple, unfortunately. Assuming that you've paid attention to the section on hygiene and used the correct storage jars (see below) then at least a year. So our official 'use by' date is one year after bottling. That's the official line but we have eaten and enjoyed chutney over three years old. We think they're like wine and improve with age.

Do use your common sense though: if you open a jar and it smells strange or off or has mould on it, don't risk eating it.

Equipment for Making Chutney

If you are set up for making jam, then you are nearly there for making chutneys. However, there are a few things to remember.

The pan should be large. A preserving pan is best, but not made of a material that will react to the acidic vinegars and give a metallic taste to the final product. Stainless steel or enamel lined pans are fine but *not* copper, aluminium or cast iron.

You will need a long-handled wooden spoon but here you are best to keep it just for chutney as it will absorb some of the spices so it could taint other foods like a jam with an unwanted spiciness.

You'll need muslin or cotton squares to hold whole spices, although we have resorted to an old pop sock once. It was clean!

The jars are important. For small quantities, jam jars are fine but for larger quantities a larger sized jar is more convenient. We find the Kilner style jars best although ours are the French Le Parfait brand that are available very cheaply in any supermarket in France when we visit. Secondhand shops, car boot sales and bring and buys can be a good source of preserving jars.

Discard any with chips or cracks to the recycling bin. If the rubber seal is looking perished, you can buy those separately from a number of online suppliers.

With ordinary jars, the covers are most important. Vinegar corrodes metal, so use plastic screw or snap-on types or the metal ones coated inside with a plastic preserving skin. If you look at a commercial jar of pickle, like Branston, you'll see the type of lid we mean. Glass lids, as used with ordinary preserving jars, are fine, of course.

Vinegar, Sugar and Spices

Vinegar is one of the most important ingredients in successful chutney making. It must be of good quality and have an acetic content of at least 5 per cent. Malt, distilled malt vinegar (white) or wine vinegar can be used. If you check on the bottle it will usually tell you the degree of acidity. This can range up to 8 per cent. If it doesn't say, assume it is lower than 5 per cent.

You can use ordinary granulated or brown sugar as you wish. Brown sugar gives a darker colour to the chutney that is often preferred. Prolonged cooking of any sugar does, however, have a darkening effect on the chutney and, if a lighter colour is wanted, the sugar should only be added when the fruit and/or vegetables are already soft and mushy.

Generally, whole spices are preferable in chutney making than ground ones, which can give a muddy appearance to the chutney, although it doesn't make a lot of difference really. Bruise these and tie them up in a muslin bag and cook with the other ingredients. However, some recipes call for a mixture of both whole and ground spices to give the best flavour.

You can make up your own pickling spices but for most chutney purposes it is far easier and gives just as good a result to buy a jar of ready mixed pickling spice.

Many of our recipes call for chillies but you need to use some judgement here. We grow our own chilli peppers and you may too. They're remarkably easy to grow in a pot on a patio or even a balcony and they're very attractive as well. What you need to be aware of is the strength of flavour. We've worked on a standard generic red chilli but you might grow *Inferno, Thai Dragon, Tabasco* or *Demon Red* to name but a few of the hundreds available. As the name suggests, they are hot, we mean really hot. You can grow chillies ten times as strong as the standard. Be careful and reduce quantities if need be or you may end up with a fiery concoction nobody can eat.

Standard Method for Making Chutney

Unlike jams where there is a fairly standard method and most recipes don't stray too far from it, with the huge range of chutneys the recipes and methods can vary greatly.

Tough or fibrous fruit and vegetables, such as onions, apples and gooseberries, should be softened in a small amount of water in a covered pan. The remainder of the cooking should be done in an open pan as evaporation of excess liquid is an important part of the cooking process.

The success of a good chutney is that it should be relatively smooth in texture and have a rich mellow flavour. To achieve this it requires long, slow cooking and then, ideally, it should be left to mature for at least three months as we mentioned above.

Tips and Things That Can Go Wrong When Making Chutney

If the chutney has shrunk in the jar, the cover is not airtight and moisture has evaporated. Always use the correct lids and, with Kilner style jars, replace the rubber rings when worn.

If loose liquid has collected on the top of the chutney, it has probably not been cooked sufficiently. It is often possible to rescue the chutney by tipping it back into the pan, bringing it to the boil again and simmering until the liquid disappears. Re-pot into cleaned and re-sterilized jars.

Don't judge the flavour of your chutney immediately. Just like freshly made wine, it will not have had chance for the flavour of the ingredients to merge and mellow. In time you will develop the ability to make some judgement as to how the flavour will turn out from the initial taste but we're still surprised at times.

Green Tomato Chutney

Makes about 2.7 kg (6 lb)

Anyone who grows their own tomatoes knows that the British summer rarely ripens all the tomatoes, although you can ripen some indoors. This versatile chutney uses those green tomatoes up. It also makes a great 'cook in' sauce for chicken as well as an accompaniment for a curry or on a cheese sandwich.

2.3 kg (5 lb) green tomatoes
450 g (1 lb) onions
1 tablespoon salt
225 g (8 oz) seedless raisins
225 g (8 oz) sultanas
28 g (1 oz) root ginger
4 red chillies
1 tablespoon whole black peppercorns
12 cloves
570 ml (1 pint) malt vinegar
450 g (1 lb) demerara sugar

Wash and finely chop the tomatoes. Peel and finely chop the onions. Place the two together in a bowl, sprinkle with the salt and leave for at least an hour.

Transfer into a pan with the raisins and sultanas. Bruise the ginger and chillies (taking care not to touch your eyes after handling the chillies) and put with the other spices into a piece of muslin, tie firmly and add to the pan with the vinegar.

Bring to the boil, then switch down to a simmer and add the sugar, stirring frequently until dissolved.

Continue stirring occasionally and press onto the muslin bag until thickened. Remove the muslin bag. Pour into hot sterilized jars and seal.

Ripe Tomato Chutney

Makes about 1.8 kg (4 lb)

It's not just the green tomatoes that you end up with a glut of. In a good year you can find you've enough tomatoes to stock a shop and this delicious chutney will take up some of the surplus.

Skinning the tomatoes is very easy. Just put them into a bowl and cover with boiling water for a few minutes. The skin will peel away very easily.

1.4 kg (3 lb) ripe tomatoes
675 g (1½ lb) cooking apples
450 g (1 lb) onions
1 tablespoon salt
855 ml (1½ pints) malt vinegar
2 teaspoons ground ginger
2 teaspoons cayenne pepper
1 teaspoon ground mixed spice
3 or 4 cloves of garlic
170 g (6 oz) soft brown sugar

Skin and slice the tomatoes, peel, core and slice the apples. Peel and finely chop the onions.

Put into a pan with the salt and half of the vinegar and heat until soft.

Add the spices (with the garlic tied in a muslin bag), stir in the sugar and the rest of the vinegar.

Bring to the boil and then reduce the heat and simmer until thick, stirring occasionally.

Pot into clean, hot, sterilized jars and seal whilst still hot. Label with contents when fully cooled.

Mango Chutney

Makes about 1.4 kg (3 lb)

This works well with a really sharp Cheddar cheese on a sandwich. One variation that added a bit of a background kick was to add a crushed dried chilli.

900 g (2 lb) mangoes
450 g (1 lb) cooking apples
1 tablespoon salt
450 g (1 lb) onions
56 g (2 oz) mixed pickling spice
1.1 litres (2 pints) distilled malt (white) vinegar
2 teaspoons ground ginger
450g (1 lb) soft brown sugar

Peel and cut the mangoes into small slices. Peel, core and slice the apples. Layer in a bowl, sprinkle with the salt and leave to steep overnight.

Rinse and drain the mangoes and apples. Peel and finely chop the onions. Put the pickling spice into a muslin bag.

Place the mangoes, apples and onions in a pan with the vinegar, ginger and bag of pickling spice.

Bring to the boil and then simmer until soft.

Add the sugar and stir until it has dissolved.

Continue simmering until the chutney thickens, stirring occasionally.

Pour into hot sterilized jars and seal.

Hot Mango Chutney

Makes about 1.4 kg (3 lb)

This is a favourite with curry, especially a super hot curry where the sweetness gives some respite when your mouth's on fire. The mixture of raisins and spices makes it more suited for a curry than the sweet mango chutney on page 117.

900 g (2 lb) mangoes
1 tablespoon salt
450 g (1 lb) onions
56 g (2 oz) root ginger
4–6 cloves of garlic
5 cm (2 inch) stick of cinnamon
170 g (6 oz) raisins
2 teaspoons hot chilli powder
1 tablespoon mustard seeds
1.1 litres (2 pints) distilled malt (white) vinegar
450 g (1 lb) soft brown sugar

Peel, halve and remove the stones from the mangoes and cut into small slices. Layer in a bowl, sprinkle with the salt and leave to steep overnight.

Rinse and drain the mangoes. Peel and finely chop the onions. Peel and finely chop the root ginger. Peel and chop the garlic. Tie the stick of cinnamon in a muslin bag.

Put all the ingredients except the sugar into a pan with the vinegar. Bring to the boil and then simmer until soft.

Add the sugar and stir until it has dissolved. Continue simmering until the chutney thickens, stirring occasionally.

Remove the cinnamon stick and pour into hot sterilized jars and seal.

Apple, Apricot and Peach Chutney

Makes about 900 g (2 lb)

This chutney always reminds us of a holiday trip to Morocco – not that chutney forms any part of Arab cuisine, as far as we know, but because of the apricot flavour.

675 g (1½ lb) cooking apples
4–6 cloves of garlic (depending on size)
112 g (4 oz) dried apricots
112 g (4 oz) dried peaches
56 g (2 oz) sultanas or raisins
2 teaspoons ground ginger
1 teaspoon cayenne pepper
2 teaspoons salt
430 ml (¾ pint) white wine vinegar
340 g (¾ lb) white sugar

Peel, core and chop the apples. Peel and crush the garlic. Cut the apricots and peaches into quarters.

Put into a pan with all the other ingredients, except the sugar, and bring to the boil. Reduce the heat and stir in the sugar, continue simmering, stirring frequently, until the chutney is thick.

Ladle into hot, clean, sterilized jars, cover and seal.

Label when fully cool.

Beetroot Chutney

Makes about 2.3 kg (5 lb)

If you like pickled beetroot, you will love this easy-to-make chutney. It works best using white vinegar and white sugar to enhance the lovely beetroot colour. If you only have large beetroot it will take a while to soften them and you may find it easiest to use a pressure cooker to initially cook them.

1.8 kg (4 lb) beetroot
450 g (1 lb) onions
6 peppercorns
6 cloves
1 lb (450 g) raisins
1 teaspoon salt
1 pint (570 ml) distilled malt (white) vinegar
1 tablespoon allspice
225 g (8 oz) white sugar

Wash the beetroot carefully without rubbing the skin and heat gently in a large pan, covering the beetroot with water, until tender.

Allow to cool, rub off the skins and dice into cubes.

Peel and chop the onions. Put the peppercorns and cloves in a muslin bag.

Put all the ingredients, except the sugar, into a large, heavy based pan.

Bring to the boil very slowly, then reduce the heat, stir in the sugar, and simmer gently until cooked and thick.

Remove the muslin bag and pour into hot, clean, sterilized jars. Seal at once. Label with contents when fully cooled.

Pumpkin Chutney

Makes about 1.8 kg (4 lb)

It's Halloween and you're carving a pumpkin to keep the children happy, so what do you do with the pulp? Of course, you could make a soup, but why not try this?

1.4 kg (3 lb) pumpkin
450 g (1 1b) ripe tomatoes
450 g (1 lb) onions
2–3 cloves of garlic
570 ml (1 pint) malt vinegar
112 g (4 oz) sultanas
2 teaspoons allspice
2 teaspoons ground ginger
2 teaspoons coarse ground black pepper
1 tablespoon salt
675 g (1½ lb) soft brown sugar

Peel and chop the pumpkin. Peel and chop the tomatoes. Peel and finely chop the onions. Peel and chop or crush the garlic.

Place the chopped pumpkin in a pan and cover with half of the vinegar, the onions, garlic, tomatoes and sultanas.

Put on a low heat and simmer for about 30 minutes until the pumpkin is soft.

Add the spices and salt and simmer for a further 15 minutes.

Stir in the sugar and remaining vinegar and continue cooking, stirring occasionally, until thick.

Allow to cool slightly, then pour into clean, sterilized jars and cover. Label with contents when fully cooled.

Hot Aubergine Chutney

Makes about 1.4 kg (3 lb)

A hot and tasty way of preserving aubergines over the winter months. Delicious with cheese but it also works well with an Indian meal.

1 kg (2 lb) aubergines
3 tablespoons salt
170 g (6 oz) soft dark brown sugar
350 ml (12 fl oz) white wine vinegar
85 g (3 oz) seedless raisins or sultanas
1 tablespoon tomato purée
450 g (1 lb) onions
3 red chillies
5 cloves of garlic
1 teaspoon cayenne pepper

Slice the aubergines, put into a colander and sprinkle with the salt. Leave for at least three hours, then rinse and dry.

Meanwhile, put the sugar, vinegar, raisins or sultanas, and tomato purée into a bowl, mix and leave to stand.

Finely chop the onions and red chillies (taking care not to touch your eyes after handling the chillies) and place with all the other ingredients into a pan.

Heat gently, stirring until the sugar is dissolved, then simmer until thickened.

Pour into hot sterilized jars and seal.

Label with contents when fully cooled.

Cucumber and Apple Chutney
Makes about 2.3 kg (5 lb)

This is one of our favourites, especially as we grow our own cucumbers and often end up with more than we can possibly eat. Ridge cucumbers, by the way, are the ones with spiky skin. You can't eat the skin but they have a superb flavour. The chutney does have a tendency to come out a little sloppy due to the water content in the cucumbers so you may need to simmer for longer than you think to get the right consistency.

If the next day you notice liquid on the top of the chutney, tip back into a pan and gently simmer the excess liquid off whilst you wash and re-sterilize the jars before re-potting.

900 g (2 lb) cooking apples
675 g (1½ lb) onions
900 g (2 lb) cucumber
570 ml (1 pint) malt vinegar
450 g (1 lb) demerara sugar
1 teaspoon salt
1 teaspoon cayenne pepper

Peel, core and chop the apples. Peel and finely chop the onions. Cut the cucumber in half lengthways and scoop out the seeds (if a ridge variety, peel as well). Chop finely.

Place the apples, onions and cucumber into a pan with the vinegar and bring to the boil and simmer until soft.

Add the sugar, salt and cayenne and stir until the sugar is dissolved. Continue simmering until the chutney thickens, stirring occasionally.

Pour into hot sterilized jars and seal. Label with contents when fully cooled.

Mixed Chutney with Mushrooms
Makes about 1.8 kg (4 lb)

The mushrooms are what distinguishes this chutney. You can use the cheapest misshaped mushrooms available in some supermarkets or you can use small whole button mushrooms, cutting the larger ones in half for a different texture.

1 largish red pepper
225 g (8 oz) onions
450 g (1 lb) mushrooms
225 g (8 oz) red tomatoes
450 g (1 lb) cooking apples
56 g (2 oz) root ginger
450 g (1 lb) soft brown sugar
225 g (8 oz) raisins or sultanas
570 ml (1 pint) malt vinegar

De-seed the pepper and chop finely. Peel and chop the onions. Put into a pan with about 285 ml (½ pint) water. Simmer to soften.

Wash and coarsely chop the mushrooms. Skin (see Ripe Tomato Chutney recipe, page 116) and chop the tomatoes. Peel and chop the apples.

Add the apples, mushrooms and tomatoes to the pepper and onions and continue cooking.

Grate the root ginger and add to the pan. Simmer until tender.

Add the sugar, raisins or sultanas and vinegar and stir until the sugar has dissolved.

Bring to the boil and then reduce to a simmer.

Continue to simmer until the chutney is thick, stirring occasionally to prevent it sticking.

Pot into hot, clean, sterilized jars immediately and seal.

Label with contents once fully cooled.

Lemon and Mustard Seed Chutney

Makes about 900 g (2 lb)

This is an unusual chutney, but it works really well and makes a great accompaniment for fish dishes. Lemon tastes good with grilled fish and this has a little of the kick you get from a tartar sauce as well.

3 lemons
1 tablespoon salt
450 g (1 lb) onions
285 ml (½ pint) white wine or cider vinegar
1 teaspoon ground mixed spice or allspice
2 tablespoons mustard seed
56 g (2 oz) raisins
225 g (8 oz) white granulated sugar

Wash, chop and remove the seeds from the lemons. Put the chopped lemons into a bowl and sprinkle with the salt. Cover with a clean cloth or kitchen roll and set aside for about 12 hours.

Peel and finely chop the onions.

In a large pan, combine the salted lemons with the onions, vinegar, mixed spice or allspice, mustard seed and raisins.

Put onto the hob and bring to the boil. Reduce the heat to low, stir in the sugar, and simmer for around 50 minutes, or until the lemons are soft and the chutney thickens, stirring occasionally.

Pour into hot sterilized jars and seal.

Label with contents when fully cooled.

Rhubarb and Ginger Chutney

Makes about 1.8 kg (4 lb)

This is nice for using up the end of season rhubarb which tends to be a little tough. The ginger flavour is distinct but not over powering.

1.4 kg (3 lb) rhubarb
450 g (1 lb) onions
112 g (4 oz) sultanas
2 teaspoons salt
2 teaspoons ground ginger
½ teaspoon ground black pepper
570 ml (1 pint) malt vinegar
450 g (1 lb) soft brown sugar

Wash, dry and trim the rhubarb and cut into 2.5 cm (1 inch) lengths. Peel and chop the onions. Put the rhubarb, onions, and all the other ingredients (except the sugar) into a pan and slowly bring to the boil.

Reduce the heat and stir in the sugar, simmer gently, stirring occasionally, until cooked and the chutney is thick.

Turn into hot, clean, sterilized jars and seal at once.

Label with contents when fully cooled.

Pear Chutney

Makes about 2.3 kg (5 lb)

If like us you grow your own chillies, instead of buying chilli powder or cayenne pepper you can take some dried chillies and whiz in the grinder attachment of a blender to make your own. Store in an airtight jar.

Drying chillies is incredibly easy. Pick with the stalk on and thread a piece of fine wire (that you can get in garden centres) through the stalk. Hang up in an airy, dry place and in a month or two you have dried chillies.

1.4 kg (3 lb) pears
450 g (1 lb) cooking apples
450 g (1 lb) onions
1 or 2 cloves of garlic
450 g (1 lb) raisins
1 teaspoon hot chilli powder or cayenne pepper
1 teaspoon ground ginger
1 teaspoon salt
½ teaspoon ground nutmeg
Juice and grated rind of 2 lemons
450 g (1 lb) soft brown sugar
570 ml (1 pint) distilled malt (white) vinegar

Peel, core and chop the pears and apples. Peel and chop the onions. Peel and crush the garlic.

Put all the ingredients, except the sugar, into a large pan with the vinegar and stir well with a wooden spoon.

Bring to the boil, stirring occasionally. Reduce to a simmer, stir in the sugar, and continue simmering for around 2 hours, stirring occasionally, or until it is thick. Ladle into hot, clean, sterilized jars, cover and seal. Label when fully cool.

Apple Chutney

Makes about 1.8 kg (4 lb)

This is a simple chutney and easy to make but nobody will believe that when they taste it. If they ask you how you made it, be mysterious and mutter about secret family recipes!

900 g (2 lb) cooking apples
225 g (8 oz) onions
225 g (8 oz) raisins or sultanas
1 teaspoon salt
855 ml (1½ pints) distilled malt (white) vinegar
56 g (2 oz) mixed pickling spice
2 teaspoons ground ginger
450 g (1 lb) soft brown sugar

Peel, core and slice the apples. Peel and chop the onions.

Put the onions, apples, raisins or sultanas and salt into a pan with the vinegar. Tie the pickling spice in a muslin bag and add to the pan. Bring to the boil and then reduce the heat and simmer until tender. Remove the spice and add the ginger.

Add the sugar, stir until it has dissolved, and continue to simmer until the chutney is thick, stirring occasionally to prevent it sticking.

Pot into hot, clean, sterilized jars immediately and seal.

Label with contents once fully cooled.

Mixed Fruit Chutney

Makes about 1.8 kg (4 lb)

The beauty of this chutney is that no two batches are exactly the same. Different types of fruit in different proportions will change the flavour a little every time.

450 g (1 lb) onions
1.4 kg (3 lb) mixed fruit – apples, pears, plums, damsons, etc
112 g (4 oz) dried dates
2 cloves of garlic
1 teaspoon salt
1 teaspoon mixed spice
1 teaspoon dry mustard
570 ml (1 pint) malt vinegar
450 g (1 lb) soft brown sugar

Peel and chop the onions. Wash, peel and core the fruits and chop into pieces. Chop the dates. Peel and crush the garlic.

Put all the ingredients into a pan (except the sugar), bring to the boil, then reduce the heat and stir in the sugar. Continue simmering, stirring frequently, until the chutney is thick.

Ladle into hot, clean, sterilized jars, cover and seal.

Label when fully cool.

11

RELISHES

Relishes tend to be half way between a chutney and a pickle. Although they use the same kinds of fruits and vegetables, the finished texture tends to be different. The fruit or vegetables are cut into small pieces or coarsely chopped and a combination of spices and flavourings is used to make them sweet, sour, spiced, etc. The preservative is the vinegar which should be above 5 per cent acetic content (as for chutneys).

Not all relishes require cooking and, those that do, take a shorter time than chutneys so that the ingredients keep their shape. This makes them quick and easy to make. You will need the same equipment as for making chutneys.

They're very versatile: some will go well with cooked meals, especially curries; and some are just right for adding a little punch to a summer salad. Relishes will mature in storage but they're usually fine to eat after just a week.

Cucumber and Green Tomato Relish

Makes 1.4–1.8 kg (3–4 lb)

A useful way to preserve those unripe tomatoes and last of the season cucumbers. A mild spiced vinegar works best for this relish.

900 g (2 lb) green tomatoes
900 g (2 lb) cucumbers
225 g (8 oz) onions
1 large green pepper
2 tablespoons salt
1 pint (570 ml) spiced distilled malt (white) vinegar
  (see page 113)
170 g (6 oz) white sugar

Chop all the vegetables finely. Put in layers in a large bowl, sprinkling each layer with the salt. Leave to stand overnight.

Tip into a colander, rinse with cold running water, and drain well.

Put the vinegar into a pan over a low heat and stir in the sugar until it has dissolved. Bring to the boil and add the vegetables.

Simmer for about 30 minutes, stirring frequently, until the mixture is fairly stiff but still moist.

Pack the relish into hot, clean, sterilized jars, right to the top.

Cover and seal immediately and label when cool.

Ready in about 4 weeks.

Hot and Spicy Red Pepper Relish

Makes about 900 g (2 lb)

You can adjust the hotness of this by varying the amount and type of chillies in the recipe.

5 or 6 red peppers (depending on size)
3 or 4 red chillies
340 g (12 oz) white sugar
170 ml (6 fl oz) red wine vinegar
285 ml (½ pint) pectin stock (see page 29)

De-seed and finely chop the red peppers. De-seed and finely chop the chillies. Take care not to touch your eyes after handling the chillies.

Mix the sugar and vinegar together in a deep pan and heat gently until the sugar has dissolved.

Add the peppers and chillies and bring to the boil. Reduce to a simmer and simmer for about 20 minutes.

Stir in the pectin stock and pour into hot sterilized jars. Seal.

Label once cool.

Ready in 3 or 4 weeks.

Chilli Pepper Relish

Makes about 900 g (2 lb)

Another relish with a chilli punch. If anything, it's a little stronger than the Hot and Spicy Red Pepper Relish.

With uncooked relishes, caster sugar tends to work better as it gives a less granular texture. You can easily make your own by whizzing ordinary granulated sugar through a food processor.

1 small cucumber
450 g (1 lb) onions
450 g (1 lb) cooking apples
12 dried chillies
1 tablespoon salt
225 g (8 oz) caster sugar
285 ml (½ pint) distilled malt (white) vinegar

Peel the cucumber and onions and finely chop. Peel, core and finely chop the apples.

Put the cucumber, onions and apples into a bowl. Crush or finely chop the chillies and add to the bowl and mix the ingredients together.

Mix the salt, sugar and vinegar in a large jug and stir until the sugar has dissolved.

Pack the vegetable mixture into dry, clean, sterilized jars without cooking.

Pour the vinegar into the packed jars until full.

Cover, seal and label.

Best kept for 3 weeks before use.

Sweetcorn and Pepper Relish
Makes about 1.8 kg (4 lb)

We don't quite know why, but a barbecue without a sweetcorn relish just isn't a barbecue. It works even better with vegetarian bean burgers that can be a little drier than beef burgers.

1 litre (1¾ pints) white wine or cider vinegar
225 g (8 oz) white sugar
1 teaspoon salt
½ teaspoon ground cloves
1 tablespoon dry mustard
1 teaspoon turmeric
450 g (1 lb) white cabbage
450 g (1 lb) onions
2 medium green peppers
2 medium red peppers
900 g (2 lb) sweetcorn kernels
1 tablespoon cornflour

Put the vinegar, sugar, salt, ground cloves, mustard and turmeric into a large pan and bring to the boil.

Finely chop the cabbage, onions and peppers. Add them with the sweetcorn to the vinegar mixture.

Bring back to the boil and stir in the cornflour.

Simmer for about 30 minutes, stirring frequently, until fairly thick.

Ladle into hot, clean, sterilized jars, cover and seal.

Label when fully cool. Ready in about 3 weeks.

Mustard Relish

Makes about 1.8 kg (4 lb)

Another relish for the barbecue and it also goes very nicely with hot-dogs.

The flavour improves if kept for at least 6 weeks before using. Make it late September/early October when the cooking apples are ready – it'll be just right for Christmas then.

1.4 kg (3 lb) cooking apples
450 g (1 lb) onions
1.1 litres (2 pints) distilled malt (white) vinegar
1 tablespoon mustard seeds
2 teaspoons dry mustard powder
225 g (8 oz) sultanas
1 tablespoon salt
450 g (1 lb) white sugar

Peel, core and chop the apples. Peel and finely chop the onions. Put the apples, onions and half of the vinegar in a pan. You can either tie the mustard seeds in a muslin bag or add them direct into the mixture.

Heat through gently and simmer until tender.

Mix the dry mustard with the rest of the vinegar and add with the sultanas and salt to the pan.

Bring to the boil, reduce the heat and stir in the sugar. Continue simmering, stirring occasionally, until thick.

Remove the mustard seeds if you have them tied in muslin and pot into dry, clean, sterilized jars and cover. Label when cool.

Beetroot and Cabbage Relish
with Horseradish

Makes about 1.8 kg (4 lb)

Follow the instructions on page 190 for dealing with horse-radish. This relish has got more kick than you might think. The amount of horseradish can be varied depending on whether you like it strong or mild. Try adding a teaspoon of dry mustard as well.

900 g (2 lb) beetroot
900 g (2 lb) white cabbage
56 g (2 oz) horseradish
225 g (8 oz) white sugar
570 ml (1 pint) distilled malt (white) vinegar
1 teaspoon salt
1 teaspoon white pepper

Wash the beetroot carefully without rubbing the skin and heat gently in a large pan, covering the beetroot with water, until tender. Allow to cool a little, then peel and chop into small chunks.

Core and shred the cabbage finely, wash and drain well.

Peel and grate the horseradish and put into a pan with the beetroot, cabbage, and other ingredients.

Mix well and gradually bring to the boil, stirring until the sugar has dissolved.

Reduce the heat and simmer for about 20 minutes until fairly thick but still moist.

Pot into dry, warm, clean, sterilized jars and cover.

Curry Relish

Makes about 1.4 kg (3 lb)

Strangely this doesn't work well with a curry but it really brightens sausages up. A hot spiced vinegar works best.

225 g (8 oz) aubergines or courgettes
225 g (8 oz) onions
225 g (8 oz) carrots
225 g (8 oz) cauliflower
112 g (4 oz) sweetcorn kernels
112 g (4 oz) peas (weight after podding)
1 tablespoon salt
140 ml (¼ pint) water
430 ml (¾ pint) spiced white wine or cider vinegar (see page 113)
170 g (6 oz) soft dark brown sugar
1 teaspoon coriander seeds
1 teaspoon ground ginger
2 teaspoons curry powder (hot or mild depending on your taste)
1 tablespoon cornflour

Wash and dice the aubergines or courgettes. Peel, wash and grate or finely chop the onions and the carrots. Break the cauliflower into very small florets. Pod the peas if you're using fresh.

Put the above into a bowl along with the sweetcorn kernels and salt and mix together. Cover with water and leave to stand overnight.

Rinse and drain well through a colander, pushing down to remove as much of the water as possible.

In a large pan, heat the vinegar and stir in the sugar, coriander, ginger and curry powder. Bring the pan to the boil and stir in the vegetables. Reduce the heat and simmer for about 15 minutes until the vegetables are just tender.

Blend the cornflour with 2 tablespoons of water and stir into the pan. Bring back to the boil and boil for 2–3 minutes or until the mixture thickens.

Pour into dry, clean, warm, sterilized jars.

Cover and seal.

Label when cool.

Best kept for at least a month before using.

Ripe Tomato Relish

Makes about 2.3 kg (5 lb)

This uncooked relish has a really fresh summery taste.

1.8 kg (4 lb) ripe tomatoes
675 g (1½ lb) onions
1 tablespoon salt
3 large celery sticks
1 large red pepper
450 g (1 lb) caster sugar
1 tablespoon mustard seeds
430 ml (¾ pint) distilled malt (white) vinegar

De-skin the tomatoes and onions and chop finely.

Mix together in a bowl and sprinkle the salt over the top. Leave overnight.

Rinse the tomatoes and onions through a colander and drain well.

Clean and finely chop the celery. De-seed and finely chop the pepper. Mix together in a large bowl with the sugar, mustard seeds and vinegar.

Stir in the tomatoes and onions.

Pot into dry, clean, sterilized jars and cover.

Label with contents.

This needs to be kept for about 6 weeks before using.

Tomato and Pepper Relish

Makes about 2.3 kg (5 lb)

Similar to the Ripe Tomato Relish but this time we are going to partially cook the ingredients.

1.8 kg (4 lb) ripe tomatoes
900 g (2 lb) onions
1 tablespoon salt
2 medium sized peppers, red or yellow
1 tablespoon mustard seeds
225 g (8 oz) white sugar
450 ml (16 fl oz) white wine or distilled malt (white)
    vinegar

Peel and finely chop the tomatoes and onions. Mix together in a bowl, sprinkle with the salt and leave overnight if possible.

Next day put the tomatoes and onions into a sieve or colander, rinse with cold running water and drain well.

De-seed and finely chop the peppers.

Mix the peppers, mustard seeds, drained tomatoes and onions in a bowl.

Mix the sugar and vinegar together in a deep pan and heat gently until the sugar has dissolved and then bring to the boil.

Add the contents of the bowl, reduce the heat, and simmer for about 10 minutes.

Pour into hot sterilized jars and seal. Ready in about 4 weeks.

12

PICKLES

Pickles can range from the simple single ingredient pickle to quite complex mixed pickles like Piccalilli. The final flavour, especially with the simple pickles, will depend heavily on the vinegar used. Even if you're a curry fan who enjoys a red-hot Vindaloo, try not to over spice and overwhelm the flavour of the ingredients.

Having said that, some people love a pickled onion that blows your head off!

Pickled Onions

If you grow your own onions then the traditional variety to grow for pickling is the Paris Silverskin. However, the commercial producers of pickled onions use Brown Pickling SY300 which you can buy seed for from most merchants.

Of course, you're not limited to these varieties. You can grow ordinary bulb onions at a close spacing – about 2.5–5cm/1–2 inches apart each way on ground that is not too rich which will result in small strong flavoured bulbs. Ailsa Craig do well like this. You can also pickle shallots in exactly the same way.

Because onions have a pretty strong flavour you can go as wild as you wish with the vinegar, even adding extra chillies to the hot flavour spiced vinegar if you are brave enough. Shallots are a little milder than onions generally, so hold back a bit on the chillies.

1.4 litres (2½ pints) water
450 g (1 lb) salt
1.4 kg (3 lb) pickling onions or shallots
Approx 570 ml (1 pint) spiced vinegar (see page 167)

Make a brine by boiling the water and salt together in a pan until all the salt has dissolved. Leave until quite cold before using.

Put the unpeeled onions into the brine and soak overnight – using a plate or something similar to keep the onions below the surface of the brine.

Drain and peel, then put into some fresh brine and soak again for a day or two.

Rinse well.

Pack into clean, sterilized jars and cover with cold spiced vinegar.

Cover and label with contents and date.

Leave for a couple of months before using. If you want a sweeter pickled onion, add a teaspoon of white sugar to each jar of onions.

Pickled Eggs

The traditional pub and chip shop delicacy is very easy to make for yourself. Obviously you need a large wide-necked jar. A 0.75 litre or even 1.5 litre Kilner style jar is ideal as it can be re-sealed as you remove the eggs.

If you keep hens and have a glut, this is an ideal way to handle some of the surplus. To decide on the quantity of vinegar that you need to heat, carefully fill a jar with shelled eggs. Fill with water and tip out into a measuring jug and add about 10 per cent.

It doesn't matter if you are an egg short as long as you have enough vinegar to cover.

Hard boiled free-range eggs (best if the eggs are at least 5 days old as, before that, they are difficult to peel)

Spiced vinegar (see page 167); tends to work best with mild spiced vinegar. If you use the mild spiced vinegar, doubling the normal quantity of cloves works well with eggs.

To hard boil the eggs, place them into a saucepan of cool water and then bring to the boil, stirring the eggs gently during the first few minutes of boiling. This helps ensure the yolks are centralized.

Boil for about 8–10 minutes and then plunge into cold water immediately to prevent the yolks getting a black ring around them. Heat the vinegar on the hob.

Remove the shells and pack the eggs into clean, sterilized jars. Pour over the hot spiced vinegar. Cover and label and store when cold.

Allow about 3 weeks for the vinegar flavour to permeate the eggs.

Pickled Cucumber

Cucumbers
Salt
Spiced vinegar (see page 167)

Wash the cucumbers and wipe clean. Do not peel unless they are bitter or a variety with a spiky skin.

Cut into slices or dice into cubes.

Layer with salt in a basin, finishing with a layer of salt.

Leave for 24 hours which will extract a lot of the moisture from the cucumber.

Rinse thoroughly in cold water and drain well.

Pack into clean, sterilized jars and cover with hot spiced vinegar.

Cover and label with contents and date.

Best if left for 4 weeks before using.

Pickled Beetroot

Beetroot
Water
Spiced vinegar (see page 167)

Wash the beetroot carefully without rubbing the skin.

Heat gently in a large pan, covering the beetroot with water, until tender. The length of time will depend on the size of the beetroot.

Allow to cool and then rub off the skins.

Large beetroot can be cut into slices of about 0.5 cm (¼ inch) or diced into cubes, small ones can be left whole. We find small ping pong ball sized beetroot best.

Pack into clean, sterilized jars and cover with hot spiced vinegar.

Seal and label with date and contents.

Using hot spiced vinegar makes the storage life longer and retains the colour.

Pickled Red Cabbage

Red cabbage
Salt
Spiced vinegar (see page 167)

Cut off and discard the outer discoloured leaves from the cabbage.

Quarter and remove the tough inner stalk. Shred the cabbage, wash and drain well.

Layer in a basin with salt between layers, ending with a layer of salt.

Leave for 24 hours which will extract liquid from the cabbage.

Wash thoroughly in cold water and drain well.

Pack into clean, sterilized jars and pour in cold, spiced vinegar.

Cover the jars and label with contents and date.

Ready after 1 week but if you keep it longer than 10–12 weeks it will lose its crispness. You can use the same recipe for Pickled White Cabbage.

Red Cabbage and Onion Pickle

Makes about 1.4 kg (3 lb)

675 g (1½ lb) red cabbage
225 g (8 oz) pickling onions
85 g (3 oz) salt
570 ml (1 pint) red wine vinegar
56 g (2 oz) white sugar
1 medium piece of root ginger
1 cinnamon stick
4 cloves
¼ teaspoon allspice
6 black peppercorns

Cut the cabbage into quarters, wash well. Cut away the tough inner core and then shred the cabbage into 1 cm (½ inch) shreds. Peel the onions and leave whole.

Layer the cabbage and onions in a bowl with the salt. Leave for 24 hours.

Rinse thoroughly in cold water and drain well. Pack into hot, clean, sterilized jars.

Put the vinegar and sugar into a pan. Roughly chop the root ginger, break the cinnamon stick, and put into a small muslin bag with the other spices. Tie and add to the pan.

Bring to the boil and then simmer for about 15 minutes. Allow to cool slightly and then pour over the cabbage and onions.

Cover and seal. Label when cool.

Ready after 1–2 weeks and goes particularly well with all type of sausages.

Beetroot and Horseradish Pickle

Makes about 1.2 kg (2½ lb)

900 g (2 lb) beetroot
56 g (2 oz) horseradish
570 ml (1 pint) spiced red wine vinegar (see page 167)
56 g (2 oz) white sugar

Wash the beetroot carefully without rubbing the skin.

Heat gently in a large pan, covering the beetroot with water, until tender. The length of time will depend on the size of the beetroot.

Allow to cool, rub off the skins and dice into smallish pieces.

Grate the horseradish and pack into hot, clean, sterilized jars with the chopped beetroot.

Heat the vinegar and dissolve the sugar into it.

Pour the hot vinegar over the beetroot and horseradish.

Cover and seal immediately.

Label when cool.

Pickled Peppers

Makes about 1.4 kg (3 lb)

900 g (2 lb) green peppers
340 g (¾ lb) onions
28 g (1 oz) dried root ginger
12 black peppercorns
3 dried chilli peppers
56 g (2 oz) white sugar
1 tablespoon salt
570 ml (1 pint) distilled malt (white) vinegar
3 or 4 cloves of garlic
1 teaspoon mustard seeds

Cut the tops off the peppers, de-seed and chop. Peel and finely chop the onions.

Bruise the ginger and tie it up in a muslin bag with the peppercorns and chillies and place in a pan with the sugar, salt and vinegar. Bring to the boil, stirring until the sugar has dissolved.

Add the peppers and onions to the pan and reduce to a simmer. Simmer gently until just tender.

Cut the garlic cloves into thin slices.

Discard the spices, remove the peppers with a slotted spoon and pack into clean, hot, sterilized jars with the thin slices of garlic and the mustard seeds.

Pour the hot vinegar over the peppers.

Cover and seal immediately.

Label when fully cool. Ready in 6 weeks.

Mixed Pickle

**Equal quantities of cauliflower, cucumber, marrow,
  French beans**
A few shallots
Salt
Spiced vinegar (see page 167)

Wash and drain the vegetables.

Break the cauliflower into small sprigs, peel (if bitter or a
ridge variety with spiky skin) and dice the cucumber, peel
the marrow and dice into cubes, trim and slice the French
beans.

Peel the shallots and leave whole.

Put into a bowl in alternate layers with salt and leave to
soak for 24 hours.

Rinse under cold water and drain thoroughly. Pack into
clean, sterilized jars and pour in cold, spiced vinegar.

Cover the jars and label with contents and date.

For an extra kick, add 1 dried chilli pepper to each jar.

Ploughman's Pickle

This is probably the most popular pickle in Britain, well known under the Branston brand name, although the exact recipe of Branston seems to be a closely guarded secret. There are numerous variations on this recipe and we would encourage you to experiment with the ingredients to achieve the result you personally like best.

Variations include replacing the gherkins with more apple and/or courgettes, adding sultanas, adding small sprigs of cauliflower or romanesco and adding very small whole onion bulbs.

If the colour seems a little pale, you can add a tablespoon of dark treacle to darken. If it still seems soft after the vegetables are softened, instead of over-boiling, try adding a little cornflour to thicken.

285 g (10 oz) carrots
285 g (10 oz) swede or turnips – young turnips tend to soften faster
2 medium onions – approximately 225 g (8 oz)
2 medium cooking or dessert apples – approximately 225 g (8 oz)
15 small gherkins
150 g (5½ oz) dates
6 cloves of garlic
250 g (9 oz) dark brown sugar
500 ml (17 fl oz) malt vinegar
4 tablespoons lemon juice
1 tablespoon Worcestershire Sauce
2 teaspoons mustard seeds
2 teaspoons ground allspice
1 teaspoon cayenne pepper
1 teaspoon salt
4 crushed cloves

Dice all the fruit and vegetables into small cubes (about 0.5cm/¼ inch is about right), crush or very finely chop the garlic.

Place all the ingredients into a large pan and slowly bring to the boil.

Simmer until the carrots and swede are soft, between ½–2 hours.

If you simmer too vigorously and the pickle begins to dry before the vegetables have softened, add a little water as you go along.

Pot into clean, sterilized jars, cover and seal.

Label with contents and date when cool.

It usually only takes a month for the flavour to mature.

Hot Piccalilli

Makes about 1.4–1.8 kg (3–4 lb)

There's no absolute right way to make piccalilli; our own recipe varies according to what we have available. Romanesco works well in place of the 'traditional' cauliflower. The only constant seems to be the use of turmeric to impart the distinctive yellow colour.

A combination of most vegetables can be used for Piccalilli but root vegetables don't tend to work very well. Pick from cauliflower, crisp cabbage, celery, cucumber, courgettes, French and young runner beans, green tomatoes, marrow, peppers, pickling onions, shallots and sweetcorn kernels. These need to be cut into fairly small pieces.

1.4 kg (3 lb) of prepared mixed vegetables
225 g (8 oz) salt
2 teaspoons turmeric
4 teaspoons dry mustard powder
4 teaspoons ground ginger
84 g (3 oz) white granulated sugar
570 ml (1 pint) distilled malt (white) vinegar
2 tablespoons cornflour

Put the mixed vegetables in a bowl in alternate layers with the salt and leave overnight.

Next day rinse in cold water and drain thoroughly.

Put most of the vinegar into a pan and add the spices and sugar and bring to the boil.

Add the vegetables and simmer the mixture until the vegetables are still crisp.

Blend the cornflour with the remaining vinegar and stir into the vegetable mixture.

Boil for 2–3 minutes, stirring gently.

Pack the vegetables into hot, clean sterilized jars using a slotted spoon. **Tip:** It's better to use wide necked jars like the 450 g (1 lb) Kilner type jars as packing them can get a bit messy!

Top up with any remaining sauce.

Cover and seal immediately.

Label once fully cool.

Ready in about 4 weeks.

Tangy Piccalilli

Makes about 2.7 kg (6 lb)

Another variation on the traditional piccalilli, not so hot as the previous.

900 g (2 lb) green tomatoes
1 large cauliflower
450 g (1 lb) shallots
2 cucumbers
450 g (1 lb) French beans
Salt
225 g (8 oz) soft brown sugar
12 g (½ oz) mild curry powder
12 g (½ oz) turmeric
28 g (1 oz) mustard
3 tablespoons cornflour
1.1 litres (2 pints) distilled malt (white) vinegar

Wash and wipe the tomatoes, cut into quarters.

Break the cauliflower into small sprigs. Wash and drain well.

Peel the shallots and leave whole.

Peel, cut and dice the cucumbers.

Top and tail the French beans and cut into 2.5 cm/1 inch lengths.

Put all the mixed vegetables into a bowl in alternate layers, with a generous sprinkling of salt and leave overnight.

Wash thoroughly in cold water and drain well.

Mix the sugar, curry powder, turmeric, mustard and cornflour into a smooth paste with some of the cold vinegar.

Heat the remainder of the vinegar in a large pan and pour onto the mixed curry powder, etc.

Return to the pan and bring to the boil.

Add the drained vegetables, reduce to a simmer, and cook the vegetables for 3–4 minutes until slightly cooked but still crisp.

Turn into clean, hot, sterilized jars and cover.

Label with contents and date when fully cooled.

Ready in about 4 weeks.

Cauliflower and Tomato Pickle

Makes about 2.3 kg (5 lb)

2 medium-sized cauliflowers
675 g (1½ lb) firm tomatoes
450 g (1 lb) onions
1 medium-sized cucumber
2 or 3 tablespoons salt
1 teaspoon dry mustard
225 g (8 oz) soft brown sugar
570 ml (1 pint) spiced white wine vinegar (see page 167)

Separate the cauliflowers into florets. Quarter the tomatoes. Peel and coarsely chop the onions. Peel and coarsely chop the cucumber.

Arrange the vegetables into layers in a large, deep dish, sprinkling equal amounts of salt on each layer. Pour over just enough cold water to cover the vegetables. Cover the dish and leave it to stand overnight.

Place the vegetables into a large colander and rinse them thoroughly under cold running water to remove excess salt. Allow to drain.

Transfer the vegetables into a large saucepan and sprinkle over the mustard and sugar. Pour over the vinegar.

Bring to the boil, stirring frequently, until the sugar is dissolved.

Reduce the heat and simmer, stirring occasionally, for 15–20 minutes.

Remove from the heat, strain off the vinegar/sugar mix into a jug and pack the vegetables into clean, hot, sterilized jars.

Pour in enough of the cooking liquid to fill each jar.

Cover immediately but leave labelling with contents and date until fully cool.

Ready to eat in about 4–6 weeks.

Damson Pickle

Makes about 2.3 kg (5 lb)

Traditionally this is made with whole damsons but we prefer it made this way. If you do use whole damsons, they should be pricked before cooking to stop them shrivelling and drying up. Just remember that stone when you come to eat it!

1.8 kg (4 lb) damsons
1 tablespoon cloves
2 or 3 blades of mace
7.5 cm (3 inch) cinnamon stick
5 cm (2 inch) root ginger
1 tablespoon allspice berries
Rind of ½ a lemon
900 g (2 lb) white sugar
570 ml (1 pint) white wine vinegar

Wash, halve and stone the damsons.

Tie the cloves, mace, cinnamon, ginger, allspice berries and lemon rind in a muslin bag.

Put the sugar and vinegar into a large stainless steel or enamelled pan and heat until the sugar has dissolved.

Bring the syrup to the boil, add the damsons and bag of spices.

Simmer for about 5 minutes or until the damsons are just soft.

Remove the damsons using a slotted spoon and pack them into clean, hot, sterilized jars.

Boil the syrup until it has reduced by about one third.

Discard the bag of spices and pour the syrup over the damsons, allowing the syrup to filter through.

If necessary add more syrup until the jars are full.

Cover and seal.

Label with contents and date once the jars are fully cool.

Ready in about 4 weeks.

Bottle any remaining syrup as the damsons may need topping up during storage.

Pickled French Beans

Makes about 1.8 kg (4 lb)

225 g (8 oz) onions
1 litre (1¾ pints) white wine vinegar
112 g (4 oz) demerara sugar
1½ teaspoons salt
4 cloves of garlic, peeled
2 bay leaves
6 black peppercorns
2 teaspoons dill seed
900 g (2 lb) French beans

Peel and thinly slice the onions and, in a medium size stainless steel or enamelled saucepan, mix them with the vinegar, sugar, 1 teaspoon of the salt, peeled garlic cloves, bay leaves, peppercorns and dill seed.

Heat on the hob and gradually bring the liquid to the boil. Reduce the heat to low, cover the pan and simmer for about 30 minutes.

Top and tail the beans and half fill another medium-sized saucepan with water and bring to the boil. Add the remaining salt and the beans, turn down the heat and simmer for 3–5 minutes. Remove the pan from the heat and drain the beans.

Put the beans, upright, into dry, clean, sterilized jars and set aside.

Remove the vinegar mixture from the heat. Strain. Pour into the jars over the beans up to the top of the jars. Cover and seal. Label with contents and date once fully cool. Store in a cool, dark place until required.

Gooseberry Pickle

Makes about 2.7 kg (6 lb)

2.3 kg (5 lb) gooseberries
450 g (1 lb) sugar
1.1 litres (2 pints) sweet spiced white wine vinegar
  (see page 170)

Top and tail the gooseberries, rinse and drain well.

In a large pan, dissolve the 450 g (1 lb) sugar into the vinegar. (This recipe needs 1.4 kg (3 lb) of sugar in total but there is already 900 g (2 lb) in the vinegar.)

Add the gooseberries to the vinegar and simmer, covered, over a gentle heat until just soft. Avoid squashing them.

Remove the gooseberries with a slotted spoon and pack into clean, hot, sterilized jars.

Bring the vinegar to the boil and reduce until thick.

Pour over the gooseberries until the jars are full.

Cover and seal.

Label with contents and date once the jars are fully cool.

Ready after about 4 weeks.

Apricot or Peach Pickle

Makes about 2.3 kg (5 lb)

1.8 kg (4 lb) apricots or peaches
1.1 litres (2 pints) sweet spiced white wine or distilled
malt (white) vinegar (see page 170)

Wash, halve or quarter the apricots or peaches (depending on size) and remove the stones. There's no need to peel them unless you don't like the texture.

Heat the vinegar and add the fruit. Simmer gently, covered, over a gentle heat until just tender but not mushy.

Remove the fruit with a slotted spoon and pack into clean, hot, sterilized jars.

Bring the vinegar to the boil and reduce until thick.

Pour over the fruit and cover and seal.

Ready after a month.

13

VINEGAR

Spiced Vinegar

A lot of pickles and relishes are preserved in spiced vinegars. The spices used vary enormously according to the recipe and to individual taste. We've listed on pages 169 and 170 examples of the most common combinations.

You can buy ready spiced or pickling vinegars, but making your own gives you even more control over the whole process. Cooking should be a creative art not an assembly line!

There are two methods for making spiced vinegar. The conventional method does, we think, give a slightly better result but the quick method is useful when you've none in stock and does give an acceptable result.

Don't forget you need to buy your base vinegar with a minimum acidity level of 5 per cent.

Conventional Method

Tie the spice mixture into a muslin bag and put into cold vinegar in a jar or bottle. Tightly cover and leave for 6–8 weeks, shaking or stirring occasionally. For sweet spiced vinegar, first dissolve the sugar in the vinegar, and then add the spices tied in muslin before leaving to steep for 6–8 weeks. Keep tightly covered.

Quick Method

Place the vinegar and the spices (tied in a muslin bag) in a heatproof basin and stand the basin over a saucepan of water. Cover the basin with a plate or the flavour will be lost with evaporation. Bring the water in the pan to the boil and then remove it from the heat. Set aside for 2–3 hours to allow the spices to steep in the warm vinegar. Strain the vinegar and cool. For sweet spiced vinegar, follow the above steps, dissolving the sugar into the vinegar before setting aside to steep.

Spiced Vinegar Recipes

Each of these provides sufficient spices for
1.1 litres (2 pints) of vinegar

Mild Spiced Vinegar

¼ oz (7 g) cinnamon
¼ oz (7 g) cloves
¼ oz (7 g) mace
¼ oz (7 g) whole allspice berries
6 white peppercorns

Medium Spiced Vinegar

¼ oz (7 g) cinnamon
¼ oz (7 g) cloves
¼ oz (7 g) white peppercorns
¼ oz (7 g) dried root ginger
¼ oz (7 g) mace
¼ oz (7 g) whole allspice berries

Hot Spiced Vinegar

1 oz (28 g) mustard seeds
¼ oz (7 g) dried chillies
½ oz (14 g) cloves
½ oz (14 g) black peppercorns
1 oz (28 g) whole allspice berries

Sweet Spiced Vinegar

1.1 litres (2 pints) vinegar
900 g (2 lb) sugar
1 tablespoon (15 ml) whole allspice berries
1 tablespoon (15 ml) whole cloves
1 tablespoon (15 ml) of coriander seeds and/or 7 g
  (¼ oz) root ginger
½ cinnamon stick – about 7 g (¼ oz)
4 blades of mace and/or rind of half a lemon
Note: Use brown sugar if using brown malt vinegar, white if using distilled malt (white) vinegar or wine vinegar.

Flavoured Vinegars

As well as pickling vinegar, you can make your own speciality vinegars.

Homemade vinegars have many uses and are cheap to make. Herb and vegetable ones add interest to salad dressings and can be used in stews, soups, sauces, etc. Fruit vinegars make refreshing drinks diluted with water or soda and add flavouring to desserts. White wine vinegar is usually the best one to use for these. There was a time when wine vinegar was quite expensive in the shops but nowadays you can pick it up anywhere and it's very affordable.

Raspberry Vinegar

Makes about 860 ml (1½ pints)

Makes a refreshing drink and good for sore throats too!

The same recipe can be used for blackberries and black-currants.

Note: You can omit the sugar if you want but this vinegar still needs to be brought to the boil for 10 minutes before final bottling.

900 g (2 lb) raspberries
570 ml (1 pint) white wine vinegar
112–340 g (4–12 oz) sugar per 570 ml (1 pint) of juice
  extracted

Put the raspberries into a wide-mouthed jar and crush them lightly with the back of a wooden spoon. Cover with cold vinegar.

Tightly cover and leave for a week or so, shaking occasion-ally.

Strain through muslin or through a jelly bag, squeezing out as much juice as possible.

Measure the juice and transfer to a pan.

Add 112–340 g (4–12 oz) of sugar per 570 ml (1 pint) of juice extracted, according to taste.

Heat gently, stirring until the sugar has dissolved and then bring to the boil.

Boil for 10 minutes and pour into hot, sterilized bottles or jars and seal.

Cucumber Vinegar

Makes about 1.1 litres (2 pints)

4 large cucumbers
450 g (1 lb) onions
1.1 litres (2 pints) white wine vinegar

Peel and finely chop the cucumber and onions.

Put into a large bowl or jar and cover with the vinegar.

Leave, covered tightly, for about a week, stirring occasionally.

Strain through muslin and pour into a sterilized jar.

Seal and label.

Garlic Vinegar

Makes about 570 ml (1 pint)

10 cloves of garlic, peeled and split into halves
570 ml (1 pint) white wine vinegar or distilled white
** malt vinegar**

Put the garlic into a wide-mouthed, warm, sterilized jar.

Bring the vinegar to the boil before pouring over the garlic.

Cover tightly and leave to stand for 3–4 weeks, shaking occasionally.

Strain through muslin and pour into a sterilized jar.

Seal and label.

Chilli Vinegar

Makes about 570 ml (1 pint)

10–15 chillies (preferably red) depending on your taste
570 ml (1 pint) white wine vinegar or distilled white
malt vinegar

Trim the chillies, split open and remove the seeds. Take care not to touch your eyes after handling the chillies.

Bring the vinegar to the boil and add the chillies. Return to the boil.

Pour into a wide-mouthed, warm, sterilized jar.

Cover tightly and leave to stand for at least a month, shaking occasionally.

Strain through muslin and pour into a sterilized jar.

Seal and label.

Herb Vinegars

Makes about 570 ml (1 pint)

Pick herbs first thing in the morning just before they come into flower.

3 good handfuls of the chosen herb (basil, rosemary, sage, mint, tarragon, marjoram) or a mixture if you prefer
570 ml (1 pint) white wine vinegar

Wash the herb leaves and tender stalks, bruise with a wooden spoon and put into a wide-mouthed sterilized jar with the vinegar.

Cover tightly and leave to stand for 3–4 weeks, shaking occasionally.

Strain through muslin, pour into a sterilized bottle, adding a fresh spray of the chosen herb into the bottle before sealing.

14

KETCHUPS AND SAUCES

If you've got the bug for making your own jams and chutneys, then we hope you'll start to make your own ketchups and sauces. Some are very easy and none is more difficult than making a chutney. When you taste the difference, you'll wonder why you didn't start years ago.

Sauces are rubbed through a sieve to give a smooth mixture and then cooked again until they are thick enough not to scparate out on standing but will still pour – they thicken as they cool. Ketchups are often strained through a jelly bag to produce a smooth purée before bottling. Both are made from similar ingredients to those used for chutneys, with the preparation and method also alike.

A suitable sieve is essential, though it is a lot easier to get the right consistency with a good electric blender.

You won't need any other equipment beyond that for making chutney but some ketchups and sauces are going to be better stored in bottles rather than jars. Finding small glass bottles is becoming more difficult as the manufacturers resort to plastic which saves them money so save any you come across. One rather good bottle, especially for ketchups, is the continental lager bottle type, with a plastic cork held in a metal frame, sold as a preserving bottle in some shops and online.

Secondary Sterilizing for Sauces and Ketchups

Sauces that are made from ingredients low in acid content, for example, mushrooms and ripe tomatoes, have to be further sterilized after bottling or they may go off. To do this, place the bottles in a deep container with a false bottom, making sure they do not touch each other or the sides of the container. You need to keep the bottles off the base of the pan or the direct heat is likely to cause them to crack and you can end up with a real mess to clean up. Although you can buy purpose made sterilizers, complete with false bottom and thermostatic control, they're quite easy to improvise.

We use our ancient hi-dome pressure cooker, which comes with a metal trivet that sits on the base of the pan creating a small gap, but you can use any large deep pan – a preserving pan is fine – and use something like a metal cake rack to prevent that direct contact. We've read that you can use folded newspaper for the task but not tried that ourselves.

Fill the pan with warm water to just below the rim of the bottles and then heat the water gently. If you're using screw tops, tighten the tops and then release by half a turn. If you're using a plastic cork type of lid, leave on but loose.

You can cap off with conventional wine bottle style corks. These need to be new and then boiled for 10 minutes to sterilize and soften them before inserting part way into the bottle.

This secondary sterilization can be a bit tricky. You don't want to keep boiling the ketchup but you need to get the temperature up enough to ensure most spoilage organisms are killed off. It's more like pasteurising than sterilizing.

The temperature you are aiming for is 77° Celsius which is easy to measure with a sugar thermometer. If you don't have a sugar thermometer, then take the water to the point where small bubbles are rising from the base and slightly steaming. Hold at that temperature for 30 minutes.

Carefully remove the bottles and allow them to cool down and then tighten the screwtop or cork. Corks are not airtight so

Fig. 5 A good homemade sterilizer is a vessel deep enough to allow for covering the bottles to the caps with water, and has a false bottom of a piece of wood, a trivet or folded newspaper to stop the bottles cracking at the bottom.

you need to seal them further. You can use candle wax dripped on or the plastic sleeves designed for wine bottles that seal when heated with a hair dryer.

All in all, screw tops or the lager style bottles (also called preserving bottles and available online as mentioned above) are far easier.

Tomato Ketchup

There's hardly a kitchen in the country where you won't find a bottle of tomato ketchup, especially if there are children in the house. You can get children to eat nearly anything with enough ketchup on it!

However, a lot of parents feel guilty about it, the shop

bought tomato ketchup is quite sweet so it must contain a fair amount of sugar. Making your own puts you in control of the sugar and you can vary the recipe to make more adult versions if you wish.

Tomatoes vary, in acidity and sweetness and the ratio of solids to liquid, according to the variety. Even the same variety varies depending when in the season they are harvested, the soil in which they are grown, and the weather during the growing season. Commercial forced greenhouse tomatoes are often watery whereas home grown, naturally fed are much denser.

These variations present a problem for the commercial producer who wants to make a million bottles a year that all taste exactly the same. For the home maker, these variations add to the charm.

Although you can compensate for watery tomatoes by cooking a little longer, evaporating the excess and concentrating the tomato flavour, there is another method – partially drying your tomatoes.

Cut your tomatoes in half and lay on a baking tray in the oven, cut side up. Put the oven on its lowest setting, Gas Mark 1 or 100° Celsius and leave for about 2–3 hours. Smaller tomatoes will dry faster than large, so keep an eye on them. It takes between 6–12 hours to get tomatoes fully dried, equivalent to the sun-dried tomatoes you can buy, but you just want to concentrate their flavour and for them to be on the point of just starting to shrivel.

Using concentrated tomatoes, as we call them, does seem to deepen the flavour.

Tomato Ketchup – Basic

Makes about 1.1 litres (2 pints)

This recipe is for a lightly seasoned tomato ketchup with a good red tomato colour and flavour. Try adding a few cloves to vary the flavour or using a white wine or cider vinegar.

2.7 kg (6 lb) ripe red tomatoes
1 teaspoon celery salt
1 tablespoon salt
225 g (8 oz) granulated sugar
2 teaspoons paprika
Pinch of cayenne pepper
285 ml (½ pint) distilled (white) malt vinegar

Wash the tomatoes and chop them. There's no need to skin or remove the seeds.

Put in a pan and heat slowly until pulped, stirring occasionally.

Press through a sieve and return the purée to a clean pan.

Add the remaining ingredients and stir until the sugar has dissolved.

Bring to the boil, then reduce the heat and simmer gently until the sauce has thickened.

Pour into hot, sterilized bottles and seal.

Note: This ketchup will require secondary sterilizing as per page 178 or it will only keep for a maximum of 4 weeks. Once opened, keep in the fridge and eat within 4 weeks.

Spicy Tomato Ketchup

Makes about 570 ml (1 pint)

A more grown up version of the old favourite, this is less sweet than the basic recipe but just as satisfying on your chips.

1.4 kg (3 lb) ripe tomatoes
225 g (8 oz) onions
10–12 black peppercorns
2 teaspoons salt
2 cloves
1 bay leaf
285 ml (½ pint) distilled white malt vinegar
84 g (3 oz) granulated sugar
1 teaspoon cayenne pepper
2 teaspoons paprika
2–3 teaspoons chilli powder

Chop the tomatoes (there's no need to skin them), peel and finely chop the onions. Crush the peppercorns.

Put the tomatoes, onions, salt, cloves, crushed peppercorns, bay leaf and vinegar in a pan and simmer for around an hour until cooked and well blended.

Sieve, return to the pan and boil rapidly until thickened.

Add the remaining ingredients and stir until the sugar has dissolved. Pour into a hot sterilized bottle.

Note: This ketchup will require secondary sterilizing as per page 178 or it will only keep for a maximum of 4 weeks. Once opened, keep in the fridge and eat within 4 weeks.

Mushroom Ketchup

Makes about 1 litre (1¾ pints)

Mushroom ketchup isn't anything like tomato ketchup in consistency but is actually thin, like a Worcestershire sauce. It pre-dates tomato ketchup which we owe, in the form we all know, to Henry J Heinz who launched his tomato ketchup in 1876.

Mushroom ketchup was a Victorian favourite and the concept was brought to the West from China as something called ke-tsiap. So, as chatni became chutney, ke-tsiap became ketchup, catchup or catsup as it is still called in some countries.

Mushroom ketchup really adds a lift to any meaty soup or stew or in a marinade and we like it sprinkled on steak half an hour before grilling.

900 g (2 lb) mushrooms (preferably large, open ones)
56 g (2 oz) salt
½ teaspoon ground allspice
A pinch of ground mace
A pinch of ground ginger
A pinch of crushed cloves
A pinch of cinnamon
285 ml (½ pint) brown malt vinegar

Wash and dry the mushrooms, trim off the ends of the stalks if necessary but do not peel them. Chop into small pieces. Layer the mushrooms in the salt in a large bowl. Cover and leave for 24 hours, then rinse and drain.

Place in a pan with the remaining ingredients and bring to the boil, reduce the heat and simmer for 30 minutes.

Strain through a sieve and pour into hot, sterilized, bottles and seal.

Note: This ketchup must be sterilized as on page 178.

Brown (Houses of Parliament) Sauce

Makes about 570 ml (1 pint)

Those of a certain age will remember when any self-respecting café offered a choice of red or brown sauce. Unlike the ketchups where Heinz definitely dominated the market, with the brown sauce it was a choice between the posh HP or Daddies. Now's your chance to break into the market!

This recipe was sent to us by a friend who emigrated to the USA and couldn't face life without his HP sauce when their customs confiscated the food parcels his mum sent him. It is complicated but turns out remarkably like HP sauce.

The treacle provides the sweetness and colour. You can use brown sugar with some dark treacle to colour if you prefer or accept that it will be lighter than the commercial.

250 ml (8.5 fl oz) white wine vinegar
250 ml (8.5 fl oz) water
125 ml (4.5 fl oz) orange juice
56 g (2 oz) pitted chopped dates
1 small onion, chopped finely
1 chopped apple (you can leave the core in)
2 or 3 cloves of garlic, put through a garlic press
2 teaspoons mustard powder
25 mm/1 inch cinnamon stick, ground
½ teaspoon ground cardamom
½ teaspoon ground cloves
½ teaspoon ground black pepper
2 teaspoons salt
200 ml (7 fl oz) dark treacle
200 g (7 oz) tube tomato purée
200 ml (7 fl oz) cider vinegar

Put the white wine vinegar, water, orange juice, dates, onion, apple and garlic in a pan and slowly bring to the boil. Gently simmer for about 20 minutes.

Either push through a sieve or use a hand blender in the pan to remove any lumps.

Add the mustard, ground spices, salt, treacle and tomato purée and then simmer for about another 40 minutes.

Add the cider vinegar and return to a simmer.

Strain through a sieve, discard any pulp.

Simmer until it thickens. If you find it is staying too thin, a teaspoon or two of cornflour can correct this.

Pour into sterilized bottles. This sauce will require secondary sterilizing as per page 178. Keep in the fridge when opened.

Parliament Sauce 2

Makes about 1.1 litres (2 pints)

This is a more traditional version of brown sauce we found on the internet some years ago. Sadly the site vanished as happens but we had noted it in our trusty exercise book.

1.8 kg (4 lb) apples, peeled, cored and sliced
450g (1 lb) prunes, stoned and sliced
2 large onions, peeled and diced – about 450 g (1 lb)
1.7 litres (3 pints) malt vinegar
2 teaspoons ground ginger
1 teaspoon grated nutmeg
1 teaspoon ground allspice
1 teaspoon cayenne pepper
8 tbsp salt
900g (2 lb) sugar

Put the fruit and onions into a large pan and cover with water.

Bring to the boil, then reduce the heat and simmer until tender.

Liquidize or sieve into a large saucepan.

Add the malt vinegar, ginger, nutmeg, allspice, cayenne pepper, salt and sugar.

Cook on a low heat until reduced and thick.

Pour into sterilized bottles. This sauce will require secondary sterilizing as per page 178. Keep in the fridge when opened.

Plum Ketchup

Makes about 1.1 litres (2 pints)

Yet another variation on the brown sauce theme but not quite as darkly coloured. Still, a spicy sauce to brighten up a range of dishes.

2 kg (4 lb) plums
250 g (8 oz) onions
125 g (4 oz) currants
4 chillies
2 thumb sized pieces of root ginger
1 teaspoon black peppercorns
1 teaspoon whole allspice
570 ml (1 pint) malt vinegar
225 g (8 oz) sugar
2 teaspoons salt

Quarter the plums and remove the stones, peel and dice the onions.

Place all the ingredients except the sugar, salt and half the vinegar in a pan and simmer for 30 minutes stirring to prevent sticking.

Rub through a sieve and return to the pan.

Add the sugar, salt and remaining vinegar, then simmer for an hour or so until thickened.

Pour into sterilized bottles. This ketchup will require secondary sterilizing as per page 178. Keep in the fridge when opened.

Gooseberry Ketchup

Makes about 1 litre (1¾ pints)

This makes a fantastic gift – if only for the look on people's faces when they see your label! It's actually quite a traditional recipe and it's delicious with strong meats like venison, game birds or duck. It even spices up a humble beef burger at the barbecue.

900 g (2 lb) gooseberries (preferably slightly under-ripe)
3 large cloves of garlic
1 tablespoon salt
1 teaspoon cayenne pepper
1 tablespoon mustard seeds
855 ml (1½ pints) white wine vinegar
335 g (12 oz) demerara sugar
112 g (4 oz) sultanas

Chop the gooseberries in half and squash down on them in a pan. Crush the garlic and add this to the gooseberries, along with all the remaining ingredients.

Bring to the boil, stirring until the sugar has dissolved, then reduce the heat to a simmer and cover.

Simmer for about 30 minutes or until the fruit is very soft and has flavoured the vinegar.

Stain through a sieve and pour the liquid into hot, sterilized, bottles and seal.

Label when cool.

Tartar Sauce
Makes about 430 ml (¾ pint)

It's the traditional and ideal accompaniment for grilled fish.
Be warned, it can be a little tricky: if you let it boil, the eggs
will curdle and the sauce is lost.

170 ml (6 fl oz) whole or semi-skimmed milk
115 ml (4 fl oz) white wine vinegar
1 tablespoon white sugar
1 tablespoon French mustard
112 g (4 oz) butter
4 eggs (preferably free-range)
Salt and ground white pepper
4 teaspoons chopped capers
4 teaspoons chopped gherkins
4 teaspoons chopped parsley
4 teaspoons chopped chives
2 tablespoons lemon juice

Put the milk, white wine vinegar, sugar, mustard, butter
and eggs into a pan and add salt and pepper to taste.

Whisk together until blended and then heat gently,
whisking all the time, until the mixture thickens. Do not
allow to boil or the eggs will curdle.

Stir in the capers, gherkins, parsley and chives and allow to
warm through. Stir in the lemon juice. Pour into hot sterilized bottles or jars and seal.

Note: This will only keep for about 3 months in a refrigerator, 6 weeks in a cool, dark place and only about a week
once opened (kept in the refrigerator). It's better to split it
into 3 or 4 small jars.

Horseradish Sauce

Fresh homemade horseradish sauce is far superior to that bought in the shops but it is a lot of fuss to make just enough for one meal and it doesn't keep above a day or two so there is no point in making more than you can use in one go.

However, by using this base recipe you can get all the hard work of preparing the horseradish done in advance which means that you spend only a few minutes actually making the sauce for a traditional beef Sunday lunch.

Horseradish is very easy to grow – in fact it is harder to kill off than grow. You just plant a piece of root in that bit of the garden where nothing else grows and leave it be. In the summer, dig up a piece of the root to make your sauce for the year. You can often find horseradish growing wild as well. If you use a wild plant, only take what you need and leave the rest to grow on.

Wash well and peel the root under water. You know how onions can make you cry? Well, horseradish is more like CS gas! Cut roughly and put into a food processor or through a fine mincer. If you have some of those DIY safety goggles you can buy cheaply, it is worth putting them on and looking rather silly when processing horseradish.

225 g (8 oz) white sugar
1 teaspoon salt
285 ml (½ pint) distilled malt (white) vinegar
Grated horseradish root

Dissolve the sugar and salt in the vinegar over a low heat and allow to cool.

Take a sterilized Kilner type jar and put in a little of the minced horseradish, then pour on some syrup. When it has settled, add more horseradish and then more syrup, repeating until the jar is full.

This base of the sauce will store for up to a year in a cool dry place.

To make the actual sauce:
1 teaspoon mustard powder
Little wine vinegar
1 tablespoon horseradish sauce base
1 tablespoon thick double cream or crème fraîche

Mix the mustard powder to a paste with a little wine vinegar. Mix the resultant mustard with the horseradish sauce base, then mix with the cream.

Mint Sauce

Once again we are making a base so when you serve lamb or new potatoes you can produce a fresh mint sauce in two minutes. The base will last around six months. Because of the cooking, this is more minty than fresh mint sauce made just with mint and vinegar.

170 g (6 oz) sugar
285 ml (½ pint) malt vinegar
112 g (4 oz) mint leaves

Dissolve the sugar in the vinegar and bring to the boil for 1 minute then remove from the heat.

Wash the mint leaves, drain well and chop finely.

Add the mint leaves to the vinegar syrup and stir well.

Allow to cool completely before potting into clean jars and seal.

To serve:
Take a small amount of the base sauce and thin to the desired consistency with vinegar or for a slightly different taste with lemon juice.

Variation:
For 4 tablespoons of the basic mint sauce, add 3 chopped lettuce leaves and 1 small chopped onion as well as the extra vinegar, water, salt and pepper. Delicious with roast lamb and lamb chops.

Apple Sauce

Makes about 1.1 litres (2 pints)

This is more of a ketchup than the traditional accompaniment to roast pork. It works well with Cumberland sausage.

1.8 kg (4 lb) apples (cooking are best)
225 g (8 oz) onions
28 g (1 oz) salt
570 ml (1 pint) mild spiced vinegar (see page 167)
225 g (8 oz) sugar

Chop the apples and onions finely and put in a pan with the salt and spiced vinegar.

Bring to the boil, then reduce to a simmer and cook gently for about 30 minutes until the pulp is finely mashed.

Pass though a sieve and return to the pan. Add the sugar, stirring well, and bring back to the boil. Boil for about 5 minutes.

Allow to cool slightly and pour into a hot sterilized bottle and seal.

Chilli Sauce

Makes about 285 ml (½ pint)

Don't forget; the hotter your chillies, the hotter the eventual sauce!

170 g (6 oz) fresh chilli peppers – red, green or yellow
  or a mixture
170 g (6 oz) onions
112 g (4 oz) cooking apple
2 teaspoons dry mustard
1 teaspoon salt
140 ml (¼ pint) distilled (white) malt vinegar

Remove the stalks and seeds from the chillies and chop as finely as possible. (Take care not to touch your eyes after handling the chillies.)

Finely chop the onions. Core, peel and chop the apple.

Put the chillies in a pan with all the rest of the ingredients. Heat gently, stirring until the mixture boils.

Turn down the heat and simmer until all the ingredients are soft and mushy and the sauce has thickened. (Takes about 40 minutes.)

Sieve and pour immediately into a hot sterilized bottle and seal.

Label once cool.

Tip: Chilli Sauce has a habit of separating on standing so shake the bottle before use.

Cranberry Sauce

Makes about 570 ml (1 pint)

What could be better as a Christmas gift? It works well with duck, goose or chicken as well as turkey though.

450 g (1 lb) cranberries
140 ml (¼ pint) distilled (white) malt vinegar
1 teaspoon ground allspice
½ teaspoon ground cloves
½ teaspoon ground cinnamon
450 g (1 lb) demerara sugar

Wash the cranberries and put in a pan with the vinegar and spices.

Bring to the boil, then reduce the heat to a simmer and cook gently until the fruit is soft and mushy.

Add the sugar and stir until it has dissolved. Bring back to the boil and boil hard for 5 minutes.

Sieve and put into a clean pan.

Return to the boil for around 60 seconds, then pour into hot, sterilized jars or bottles and seal.

Label when cool.

15

CONVERSION CHARTS

All these are approximate conversions. When following a recipe, don't mix metric and imperial measures – stick to one system or the other.

Weights		Volume	
½ oz	14 g	1 fl oz	28 ml
1 oz	28 g	2 fl oz	56 ml
1½ oz	42 g	3 fl oz	84 ml
2 oz	56 g	5 fl oz	140 ml
3 oz	84 g	(¼ pint)	
4 oz	112 g	10 fl oz	285 ml
5 oz	140 g	(½ pint)	
6 oz	170 g	15 fl oz	430 ml
7 oz	200 g	(¾ pint)	
8 oz	225 g	1 pint	570 ml
9 oz	253 g	1¼ pints	690 ml
10 oz	280 g	1½ pints	855 ml
12 oz	340 g	1¾ pints	1 litre
13 oz	365 g	2 pints	1.1 litres
14 oz	392 g	2¼ pints	1.3 litres
15 oz	420 g	2½ pints	1.4 litres
1 lb (16 oz)	450 g	2¾ pints	1.6 litres
1¼ lb	560 g	3 pints	1.7 litres
1½ lb	675 g	3¼ pints	1.8 litres
2 lb	900 g	3½ pints	2 litres
3 lb	1.4 kg	3¾ pints	2.1 litres
4 lb	1.8 kg	4 pints	2.3 litres
5 lb	2.3 kg	5 pints	2.8 litres
		6 pints	3.4 litres
		7 pints	4 litres
		8 pints	4.5 litres
		(gallon)	

Measurements		Oven Temperatures	
¼ inch	0.5 cm	Mk 1 275°F	140°C
½ inch	1 cm	Mk 2 300°F	150°C
1 inch	2.5 cm	Mk 3 325°F	170°C
2 inches	5 cm	Mk 4 350°F	180°C
3 inches	7.5 cm	Mk 5 375°F	190°C
4 inches	10 cm	Mk 6 400°F	200°C
6 inches	15 cm	Mk 7 425°F	220°C
7 inches	18 cm	Mk 8 450°F	230°C
8 inches	20.5 cm	Mk 9 475°F	240°C
9 inches	23 cm		
10 inches	25 cm		
12 inches	30 cm		

When recipes call for a spoon measurement, this should be a level spoonful unless otherwise stated.

1 teaspoon	=	5 ml measuring spoon
1 dessertspoon	=	10 ml measuring spoon
1 tablespoon	=	15 ml measuring spoon

US RECIPE MEASUREMENTS TO
IMPERIAL AND METRIC

Flour (based on plain white)

1 cup	=	5 oz	=	140 g
½ cup	=	2.5 oz	=	70 g
¼ cup	=	1.25 oz	=	35 g

Sugar (granulated)

When a US recipe just calls for sugar, it is granulated. Caster sugar is Superfine. Icing sugar is Powdered.

1 cup	=	7 oz	=	200 g
½ cup	=	3½ oz	=	100 g
¼ cup	=	1¾ oz	=	50 g

Butter

Butter in the US comes in sticks and some recipes call for a stick of butter or margarine. This is equal to ½ a cup.

1 cup	=	8 oz	=	227 g
½ cup	=	4 oz	=	113.5 g

Fluids

1 cup	=	8 fluid oz	=	250 ml
½ cup	=	4 fl oz	=	125 ml
¼ cup	=	2 fl oz	=	65 ml

An American quart = 32 fluid oz and is 2 American pints.
An American pint is 16 fluid oz and is 2 American liquid cups.
Dessert spoons are not used in the US in recipe ingredients. A tablespoon and teaspoon are roughly the same as the UK.

All these are approximate measurements.

INDEX

Also by John Harrison

VEGETABLE GROWING MONTH BY MONTH
The down-to-earth guide that takes you through the vegetable year

John shows you when you should sow your seeds, dig your plot and harvest your crops.

- Choose appropriate vegetables for your soil
- Select the right position so that they flourish
- Make your own compost and organic fertilizers
- Use the best methods for pest control
- Extend the season with cloches and cold frames

'Harrison's book is crammed with useful information, unencumbered by any trendy graphics . . . it's perfect for all those gardeners who just want a book to tell them exactly what to do, and when.'

Emma Townshend in the *Independent on Sunday*

'Forget about any glossy pictures, what's in this book is solid words of advice, written in plain-to-understand English from a grower who's had frustrating years of experience behind him in trying to grow nutritious vegetables, whilst at the same time running a business and raising a family. Everyone will benefit from this book and I found the glossary at the back, which explains gardening terminology in a way that everyone will understand, to be extremely useful. It will certainly have a place on my extensive gardening bookshelf.'

Medwyn Williams, *Chairman of the National Vegetable Society and member of the Fruit and Vegetable Committee of the Royal Horticultural Society*

Also by John Harrison

THE ESSENTIAL ALLOTMENT GUIDE
How to get the best out of your plot

John Harrison, who has been described as 'Britain's greatest allotment authority' (*Independent on Sunday*), shows how you can enjoy the taste of real food from food grown on your allotment. Discover how to:

- Get your own allotment – top tips to help you beat the waiting list
- Clear an allotment and safely dispose of rubbish
- Plan your plot for maximum production
- Keep the children occupied and helping

LOW-COST LIVING
Live better, spend less

Reduce your living costs, lower your carbon footprint and still live well.

When economic conditions are tough, we all need to watch our spending. John Harrison's simple, tried and tested methods will help you to enjoy a better standard of living while saving money and helping the environment.

Discover the benefits of growing your own fruit and vegetables, raising chickens, making butter, cheese and bread, and brewing your own beer. Save energy, save on your bills. Harvest food for free and avoid waste. Play the supermarkets at their own game and get the best deals. See how to recycle, re-use, make do and mend. Find out if solar or wind power makes domestic sense.

You can order *Right Way* books from our website **www.constable robinson.com/rightway** or telephone the TBS order line: 01206 255 800 (Monday – Friday, 8.30 am – 5.30 pm).